Circle *of* Success

Trust
Belief
Focus
Attitude
Teamwork
Confidence
Perspective
Persistence
Commitment
Self-Respect
Self-Discipline
Responsibility

Bill Leach & Ted Newland
with
Lesley Bindloss

Hawthorne Hills Publishers
P.O. Box 5209
Irvine, CA 92616

Library of Congress Catalog Card Number: 2001126372

ISBN 0-9708642-0-5

Cover and text design - SHB Design

Dedication

To my daughter Alisha and my son Bill, who have grown into responsible and loving adults, and to my younger sons Shane and Hayden, who still have the transition to adulthood ahead of them. May this book, in whatever small way, assist you in your journey.
BL

To my mother, Joyce, who worked hard to make me tough physically, mentally, and emotionally, so I could survive in this world.
EHN

To my Dad, who inspired me with "Betsy" stories, and to my Mum, for her love.
LHB

Table of Contents

Foreword

Most of us would like to change something about our lives. So we buy a book, join a gym, or go on a diet. We are a resolution-making people. Unfortunately, we are also a resolution-breaking people, so the book sits on the shelf, we can't seem to make it to the gym, and we abandon the diet. It's the American way.

But not for all of us. There are exceptions. The exceptions deserve our attention.

I know the two exceptions that wrote this book.

Bill Leach has been a friend for many years. I heard his story in small parts - like these chapters. Bill would rather go to the dentist than tell you his accomplishments. Eventually I learned that he is an Olympian, and in 1996 he won the World Championship in triathlon for men over 50. This surprised me on a couple of fronts. First, he looks around 40. Second, he had to swim in Cleveland Harbor to win the triathlon title. That's amazing in itself. I'm from Northeastern Ohio. I know how polluted the water used to be.

Ted Newland's a different story.

A reporter friend – newspaper, not my world of television and radio– told me that Newland was an interesting guy. In fact, my buddy told me Newland was the most interesting guy he'd ever met. That's the kind of statement that gets a reporter's attention. So we set up a lunch with Newland, and before long I had cameramen following him around for a full season. Newland, I learned, is the water polo coach with the most wins in the history of the NCAA.

It also turned out that Leach and Newland knew each other. In fact, they've been working out together for over 40 years, first as player-coach, and then as best friends. Together they have probably logged more hours in training than any two people their combined age in the world. Just a guess, but a very good guess, I think.

I thought the two would have something to say to anyone who has ever wondered what it's like to be a world-class athlete, or a championship coach. Actually, they have something important to say to everyone who values success in their lives. They know about training the body, but they speak about training one's life.

No matter what you do, if you do it haphazardly, the results will disappoint. Leach and Newland have had their share of disappointments, and they discuss them in this book. But their triumphs are far more numerous. Read this book, discover what they've learned from their world of sport, and apply it to your life. You'll be happy you did.

~ Hugh Hewitt, author of **Searching For God In America** *and*
The Embarrassed Believer*; Emmy award-winning broadcast journalist.*

Acknowledgements

Special thanks to coach Al Irwin for taking Bill Leach with him to UCI, and later for bringing Ted Newland over to be swimming and water polo coach. His confidence in us shaped our lives.

To all the students and faculty at Corona del Mar High School who have assisted by typing, reading, and listening to the manuscript: Heather Archer, Jon Berg, Jocelyn Brown, Kelsey Clark, Samantha Cohen, Taylor Decker, Judd Hietbrink, Forrest Mack, Innes McDonald, Camille Packer, Chris Rothwell, Tom Scheck, and Katie Wiedemann. To Maureen Oeding and Lois Smith, who let us print selected pieces in the Mac Lab. To Principal Dr. Don Martin, for his understanding. To Alexander Niehenke, who designed the Circle of Success graphic on the dedication page, and Brian Slingsby for his insights.

Thanks to Vicki Ronaldson for her help early on, and to the many friends who read and commented on the manuscript: Evan Forbes, Jan Horn, Kaye Hawthorne, Bob Cuyler, Jim Tomlin, John Emme, Greg Leavey, Bill Lobdell, Bonnie Fullerton, Vicky Gerson, Ruth Anne Williams, Rod Jones, John Brazelton, Kathy Mohs, Ed Conway, Mike Marino, Mike Starkwether, Tina Hoover, Paul Pratt, and Olympians Chuck Bittick and Dr. Andrew Strenk. To Chuck Trevisan for his artistic advice, and to Ken McAlpine, who helped us start this project, "way back when". Thanks to Kay Sandland for her support.

To Claudia Suzanne for her brutal honesty with our initial manuscript, and to Canadian triathlete Ian Hooley, who agreed with her. To John Boston, for his enthusiasm, and for taking good care of Alisha. To Bill's long-time friend, Brad Sympson, for his valuable feedback.

A very special thanks to our spouses: Julie, Anne, and Keith, for their support during this long, long, process.

A big "thank you" to Emma and Chris Bindloss, for letting their mother "hog" the computer.

Thanks to Hugh Hewitt for first pointing us in the right direction, and later for taking the time to keep us on track.

To Suzanne Barnes, of SHB Designs, for the design and layout of the book and offering her professional advice.

To Bill Braly, for taking the photo on the back cover.

Thanks to Zanzibar, Java City, Diedrich's, and Starbucks Coffee Houses in Irvine, our favorite places for coffee and inspiration.

And, to anybody we've forgotten, sorry! We appreciate you too.

Introduction

In 1986 I turned forty, and Ted Newland was nearing sixty. I was working out every day, and so was he. We both enjoyed sport and knew that our lives were richer and our bodies healthier because of it, and it occurred to us that it was time to write a book explaining Newland's philosophy. If others knew what we knew, their lives could be enhanced too. Full of optimism, we wrote a couple of chapters of what was basically a "how to" book. I spoke with some publishers, and although they were polite, they showed little interest. In their words, "the fitness boom was over".

Time passed. For ten years, "the book" sat on a shelf. I turned fifty, and won a Triathlon World Championship for my age group. Newland had his sixty-ninth birthday, and won another NCAA Water Polo Championship. We were still working out every day. The fitness boom was still booming. In fact, fitness oriented recreation was exploding, and we realized that now we had even more to say about fitness than we had ten years before. Only this time, instead of a fitness manual, we would explain how sport had helped us develop the emotional qualities necessary for success in all areas of life. We believe that the lessons we have learned in over a hundred years of athletic experience are universal lessons. It doesn't matter that we learned most of them through a career in sports, because they apply as much to business, marriage or any other endeavor you decide to pursue.

With the assistance of Lesley Bindloss, whose writing and editing skills helped us form and express our ideas, the book began to take shape. Ironically, the strengths we acquired over many years in athletics, which we wanted to explain in the book, were the very qualities we needed to write it. We started with a dream, and then worked as a team to achieve it. We persevered in finding the right format, and did many re-writes. We used self-discipline to find the time week after week to fit the book into our busy schedules. Above all, we believed in ourselves, and we did not give up.

We have reached the finish line. We hope you enjoy the book.

~ *Bill Leach*

Chapter One

Belief

. . . .

They are able because they think they are able.
~ *Virgil*

. . . .

In the long run, men hit only what they aim at. Therefore, though they should fail immediately, they had better aim at something high.
~ *Henry David Thoreau*

. . . .

You have powers you never dreamed of. You can do things you never thought you could do. There are no limitations in what you can do except the limitations of your own mind.
~ *Darwin P. Kingsley*

. . . .

Shoot for the Moon

*If I accept you as you are, I will make you worse; however, if I treat
you as though you are what you are capable of becoming,
I help you become that.*
~ Johann Wolfgang von Goethe

Before I joined Newland's program, it was hard to imagine that
I'd ever be successful in athletics. In junior high school I was definitely a second-string "wanna-be", clumsy and overweight and usually one of the last to be picked for a team. The most logical sport for
me to try in high school seemed to be swimming, for as well as growing up with a pool in the back yard, I had spent long summer days body
surfing at the beach. My closest friends had decided to play water polo,
and I figured it would be good preparation for the swimming season,
so I signed up too. I knew nothing about the sport, or the coach.

A few days into practice a tall, bronzed, muscular man in a white t-
shirt with Newport Harbor Athletics emblazoned on it strode onto the
pool deck. His aura of quiet confidence and strength could not be ignored, and as a gangly group of fourteen-year-old boys we were in
awe. This was Newland: tough, hard to please, brilliantly charismatic.

These were the '60s, and week after week we would hear John F.
Kennedy on the radio and TV, talking about the space program as if it
were a reality. "We choose to go to the moon in this decade not because it is easy, but because it is hard, because that goal will serve to
organize and measure the best of our energies and skills, because that
challenge is one that we are willing to accept," he said in a 1962 speech
at Rice University in Houston. We understood. We had chosen to stay
on Newland's team, certainly not because it was easy, but because we
had accepted the challenge. Day after day we would listen to his voice
booming out across the water, urging us to work harder, get tougher,

. . . .

Deep within man dwell those slumbering powers; powers that would astonish him, that he never dreamed of possessing; forces that would revolutionize his life if aroused and put into action.
~ Orison Swett Marden

. . . .

It is the awareness of unfulfilled desires which gives a nation the feeling that it has a mission and a destiny.
~ Eric Hoffer

. . . .

Confidence and belief in your own abilities will get you about 85% of the distance to your goal. The coach that has confidence in those same abilities will push you the added 15% of your journey.
~ Chuck Bittick

. . . .

and achieve what we never thought possible.

Newland didn't always start with the most talented athletes, either in high school or later at the college level, but he had an incredible ability to squeeze from his players every last drop of potential. His belief that we could develop into a dominant water polo team was so strong, that eventually we too caught the vision. If it was uncomfortable to do 500 sit-ups, we took it as a challenge and did not give up. If it seemed impossible to bench press 300lbs, we learned to build up gradually, and we usually achieved our goal. Newland inspired us; we burned to live up to his expectations.

I realized early on that the only way I could develop my athletic ability was through the one talent I possessed: the ability to work hard. Newland's formula for success: hard work, belief, and a passion for excellence, helped me break through my physical and mental limitations and I became a High School All-American, then Athlete of the Year, and ultimately an Olympian. There is no question in my mind that without Newland none of these accomplishments would have occurred. Kennedy inspired us as Americans, but Newland inspired us as athletes. Both believed in us, both taught us to shoot for the moon. *BL*

Newland wouldn't have had the kind of response and loyalty from his players that he had if the program was only about working hard. There was a shared sense among us that here was a man who stood for what he believed in, and he believed in us, and our potential. It meant a great deal to know that Newland had faith in me. It made me believe in myself.

~ Michael Martin Sherrill, U.C.I. water polo team 1967-71

. . . .

I don't think that anything is unrealistic if you
believe you can do it.
~ *Mike Ditka*

. . . .

Courage is the capacity to confirm what
can be imagined.
~ *Leo Rosten*

. . . .

And what he greatly thought, he nobly dared.
~ *Homer*

. . . .

Every Achievement Starts with a Dream

All of our dreams come true, if we have the courage to pursue them.
~ Walt Disney

We all need dreams and goals. As the motivational speaker Les Brown once said: "Your goals are the road maps that guide you and show you what is possible for your life." It doesn't matter what triggers your dream, only that you have one.

When I was six or seven years old, I used to ride my bike to the local five and dime store to buy candy. My favorite was bubble gum. I loved to tear off the wrapper, bite into the sweet-tasting gum, and read the fortune at the bottom of the comic strip. I didn't usually take the "fortunes" seriously, but one day I read one that struck me differently. It simply said: "One day you will be an Olympic athlete". The Olympic Games at Helsinki had just ended, and although I knew very little about them, I knew enough to realize that the Olympics was a very special event for very special athletes. I decided then that some day I wanted to be able to call myself an Olympian.

At the time I would have been voted "least likely to become an Olympian". I had learned to ride my bike long after the other kids on the block, and was never a star in any of the sports I tried. But I could dream. I wanted the fortune to come true and I saved that wrapper, putting it in a little box with other mementoes that had meaning only for me. I kept it for years, and every once in a while I'd come across it and be reminded of its message. In high school I got involved in swimming, and when I found I was fairly good at it, I worked hard to improve, always with the words of the "fortune" in the back of my mind. By the time I was playing water polo for Newland, I firmly believed that if I worked hard enough, it was truly possible to go to the Olympics.

. . . .

There is some place where your specialties can shine. Somewhere that difference can be expressed. It's up to you to find it, and you can.
~ David Viscott

. . . .

People with goals succeed because they know where they're going.
~ Earl Nightingale

. . . .

I consider a goal as a journey rather than a destination.
~ Curtis Carlson

. . . .

Somewhere over the years I lost the box, but the message remained with me. I used it often to help me stay focused, especially when I switched my sport to kayaking with the express purpose of making the 1972 Olympic team. I didn't reach my goal until 1976, when I was thirty years old, but was it worth it? Absolutely! Looking back, it seems absurd that something as insignificant as a bubble gum wrapper could put a dream into my head, but it did. All achievements start with a dream, however humble, and I've learned that "what we can conceive, we can achieve". I hope to pass this lesson on to my children. *BL*

. . . .

How can you possibly find your boundaries unless you explore as far and as wide as you possibly can? I would rather fail in an attempt at something new and uncharted than safely succeed in a repeat of something I have done.
~ *A.E. Hotchner*

. . . .

Be like the turtle. If he didn't stick his neck out, he wouldn't get anywhere at all.
~ *Harvey Mackay*

. . . .

I had ambition not only to go farther than any man had ever been before, but as far as it was possible for a man to go.
~ *James R. Cook*

. . . .

Better to Fail, than Never to Try

*Discoveries are often made by not following instructions, by
going off the main road, by trying the untried.*
~ Frank Tyger

Newland was always trying to find ways to toughen us up so we
could make the leap to the elite level of U.S. Water Polo. Sometimes
his ideas worked, and sometimes they didn't, but he was always enthusiastic and willing to try new things.

In the early years of his coaching, Newland decided that weight
lifting could dramatically improve the strength and performance of his
players. He tested his theory by setting up his garage for lifting, and
many athletes came over regularly to work out. In those days weights
were not as available as they are now, so Newland would take lead and
melt it down, pour it into tin cans and put an "eye" bolt in the soft lead
to make pulleys. Newland was one of the first to make weightlifting a
vital part of his coaching, and the new training regimen was incredibly
successful.

One day we arrived at workout to find him surrounded by punch-
ing bags, gloves and helmets. He had recently returned from the 1968
Mexico City Olympics where he had been coaching Toni Hewitt, one
of his swimmers. While he was there he learned from some Romanian
coaches that their water polo players had been boxing each other as
part of their training. Having once been a boxer himself, the idea ap-
pealed to Newland, and he returned home eager to try this new training
plan on us.

After we had lifted weights and done stomach exercises, Newland
took us into the room next door to teach us the rudiments of boxing.
Basically, we had to learn to protect ourselves by fending off the
opponent's blows. After a couple of days he paired us up and had us
spar with each other, nothing too aggressive, just enough to get the feel

. . . .

The country needs, and unless I mistake its temper, the country demands, bold, persistent, experimentation. It is common sense to take the method and try it; if it fails, admit it frankly and try another.
But above all, try something.
~ *Theodore Roosevelt*

. . . .

Life has no limitations, except the ones you make.
~ *Les Brown*

. . . .

The ultimate creative capacity of the brain may be, for all practical purposes, infinite.
~ *George Leonard*

. . . .

of hitting and counter-punching and moving our legs to keep our balance. We learned that height and reaction time help determine boxing style. If you're taller than your opponent you stand more upright, and if you're shorter you crouch down to make yourself a smaller target. You have to protect yourself and wait for an opening to get your punches in.

With the helmets and gloves we were fairly well protected, and nobody got hurt that first week. Even direct hits to the head didn't do any damage. In fact, it was really kind of fun. The sound of gloves pounding into someone's stomach or glancing off each other is a sound you never forget.

One afternoon Newland told us it was time to box him, and the room fell silent. We sat along the wall trying hard not to be noticed, because no one wanted to go first. You could almost smell the fear. Newland had been a "Golden Gloves" champion in school, and we knew we were going to be pummeled and put in the "hurt-locker". This was precisely why he had us boxing: if we could experience pain and learn to deal with it, we would be free of the fear of being hurt and we'd do better in competition.

The first guy up was Pat McClellan, who had been Southern California Player of the Year in high school and was about 6'1" and 215 pounds. Within seconds he was sitting on the mat with a look of bewilderment on his face. When Newland hit him he was actually lifted off the floor, his legs went out in front of him and he landed with a loud thwack. He looked around at our stunned faces, and after clearing his head he wanted to know what had happened. He said he had seen the punch but hadn't felt it, and the next thing he knew he was on the mat.

Newland called up the next guy, Ferdie Massimino, who was only slightly smaller than McClellan. After some simple sparring the same thing happened, only this time we could really hear the smack of leather on skin and the thud as Ferdie ended up like Patrick, on the mat with no idea how he'd gotten there. Again, no complaint of pain, just bewilderment. We all shrank back a bit, knowing that each of us in turn would experience the same fate.

As luck would have it, I was the next victim. At 5'9" I was quite a bit shorter than Newland's 6'1", so I crouched down as low as I could without looking like I was attempting to crawl into a hole and disap-

. . . .

How far is far, how high is high?
We never know until we try.
~ *Song from the California Special Olympics*

. . . .

I've never been afraid to fail.
~ *Michael Jordan*

. . . .

Creativity is thinking up new things.
Innovation is doing new things.
~ *Theodore Levitt*

. . . .

pear. When you know what is about to happen, the adrenalin and the fear are flowing. I tried to keep my hands up to fend off his blows and for a while I was pretty successful. But his experience saw weaknesses everywhere, and he moved in for the kill. All I remember, and it seemed to be in slow motion, was his right glove coming out of nowhere headed directly for my face. I closed my eyes, knowing what was about to crash into me. My instincts must have taken over, because I don't recall what happened next, except that I opened my eyes and I was still standing. No pain because, mercifully, the glove never touched me. Instead, I saw Newland curled up in a fetal position on the floor, holding his sweats where his jock strap would be. Apparently I had reacted by driving a left upper cut right into his cup, and the right hand that was certain to connect with my face was withdrawn as quickly as it had been thrown. I felt terrible. Nothing like a blow below the belt to ruin all the fun. As Newland recovered he called the workout, and as we made our way to the locker room all the guys were thanking me and slapping me on the back. At first, I didn't understand, but then I realized that because of my "lucky" blow I had saved everyone else from their "punishment".

I think Newland realized something: that boxing with a bunch of neophytes can be dangerous. He told us later he'd decided to suspend our boxing lessons to avoid causing additional injuries. We never asked whether he was talking about injuries to us or to him; at any rate, we never put on gloves again.

Newland was undaunted by the failure of his plan, because he knew the value of being innovative and trying new things. Although our boxing experience was short lived, it strengthened the common bond of the team and a year later we won our second AAU Championship at the Indoor Nationals in New York. *BL*

While many people think that Newland is set in his ways, he has always had a willingness to take risks and experiment with new ideas. He is honest, strong, and true to himself, which is the reason I admire him, not only as a coach, but as a man.
~ John Vargas, U.C.I Water Polo, 1979-82

· ·

Oh man! There is no planet, sun or star could hold you, if you but knew what you are.
~ *Ralph Waldo Emerson*

· · · · · · · · · · · · · · ·

I am willing to put myself through anything; temporary pain or discomfort means nothing to me as long as I can see the experience will take me to a new level. I am interested in the unknown, and the only path to the unknown is through breaking barriers, an often painful process.
~ *Diana Nyad*

· · · · · · · · · · · · · · ·

When we are motivated by goals that have deep meaning, by dreams that need completion, by pure love that needs expressing, then we truly live life.
~ *Greg Anderson*

· ·

The Ironman Experience

What you get by achieving your goals is not as important as what
you become by achieving your goals.
~ Zig Ziglar

When I was new to triathlons, the one question people always asked was, "Have you done the Ironman?" All I knew about this race they called the Ironman came from an article in *Sports Illustrated* that described it as one of the toughest, most physically and mentally exhausting one-day competitions in the world. After reading with mild interest how the athletes swam 2.4 miles in the ocean, biked 112 miles, and then topped it off with a 26.2 mile marathon, I decided that it was definitely not an event for the fainthearted, and put the magazine down. Only several months later did I realize, a little apprehensively, that if I wanted to gain recognition in the world of triathlon competition, I too would have to accept the challenge of the Ironman. Thus began one of the greatest experiences of my life.

Most people think of Hawaii as a lush tropical paradise, with huge tree ferns, waterfalls, and exotic flowers, and I was no exception. I had heard stories about the brutal terrain and inhospitable environment of the Ironman, but hardly believed them until I saw the course for myself. I was surprised to find that it cuts across what is basically a lava field along the Kona coast of the big island of Hawaii. Black, razor-sharp rocks stretch for miles on either side of the King Kamahamaha Highway, and the intense heat and humidity, combined with strong winds that blow almost continuously along the Kona coast, make it clear why athletes who've done the race command such respect from the sporting community.

Today there is an elaborate series of qualifying races that makes it hard even to enter the Ironman; back in those days all you did was fill out the application, send in the entry fee, and you were in. I decided

. . . .

*Champions know there are no shortcuts to the
top. They climb the mountain one step at a
time. They have no use for helicopters!*
~ *Judi Adler*

. . . .

*Dreams can often become challenging, but
challenges are what we live for.*
~ *Travis White*

. . . .

*Life's challenges are not supposed to paralyze
you, they're supposed to help you discover
who you are.*
~ *Bernice Johnson Reagon*

. . . .

that I would compete in the race in February of 1982, and once I'd made the decision I was completely committed to it. My job as a history teacher left me more time to train than many careers would have, and although there was always something I would rather do than train, each day I'd make the decision to get out there, regardless. To be successful, I knew I needed to be proficient in all three sports, and I had months of workouts ahead of me.

I remember Newland saying that self-discipline would take us a long way, but to ensure my commitment I bought a $1000 "used" racing bike, figuring that if I invested what in those days was a huge amount of money, I'd have to go out and train to justify the expense. Sometimes these little tricks help get the job done.

I trained as hard as I could, and on paper my personal bests convinced me I could be a contender in this race. I was ready, or so I thought. You never know how things will turn out on the day of the race.

On the morning of the competition I stood on a sliver of sandy beach with about 700 other athletes, waiting to swim 2.4 miles in the Bay of Kailua Kona. Surprisingly, I was not nervous. I was fresh, pumped with adrenalin, and expected the swim to be the easiest part for me since I'd been a distance swimmer in college. Conditions were good, although it was a little disconcerting to look down through my goggles and realize that the tiny black squiggles I could see in the clear water were actually sharks, big sharks, circling in the ocean 100 feet below me.

I came out in the lead pack and mounted my bike in 4th place. Both the bike and the running segments of the race are out and back along the same road, and as I rode, hour after hour, my quad muscles began to burn. Fatigue set in, and my spirits started to flag. I had expected the race to be physically exhausting, even for a well-trained athlete, but I was surprised at how much of a challenge it was mentally. 112 miles on a bike is a long way. I hadn't realized how alone I would feel out there on the course, for although I saw a few friends along the way, we couldn't help each other. I realized we were all in our own little world, struggling to conquer the demons of the racecourse: discouragement, fatigue, fear of failure, and the oppressive heat of an ever-present sun.

I knew I would never quit, for taped to my handlebars was the name Frank Sanborn. One of my best friends and kayak training part-

. . . .

Difficulties increase the nearer we
approach the goal.
~ *Johann Wolfgang von Goethe*

. . . .

Self-confidence is the result of a successfully
survived risk.
~ *Jack Gibb*

. . . .

Permanence, perseverance, and persistence in
spite of all obstacles,
discouragements, and impossibilities:
it is this, that in all things
distinguishes the strong
soul from the weak.
~ *Thomas Carlyle*

. . . .

ners, Frank had been playing basketball just a few months previously when he collapsed after grabbing a rebound, and although the paramedics arrived within a couple of minutes, he died right there on the court. He was 21 years old. As a gesture of respect and a tribute to my friend, I wanted to race this first Ironman for him. I was determined not to quit until I had crossed the finish line, but it was tough. Not only did I have to contend with mental and physical depletion, but the race conditions were as brutal as I'd been told they'd be. There was no shelter for 52 miles along the highway, just black lava rocks sucking up the sun's heat and belching it back into my face as I biked along this interminable stretch of road. The wind blew relentlessly, often slowing me from as much as 40 miles an hour down to 8 or 10 miles per hour. Sudden gusts of wind flung lava pellets against my helmet over the last few miles to the turn-around point at Hawi, and just when I was thinking with relief how much easier it would be on the way back with the downhill and a tailwind to help me, the unpredictable breeze whipped around and was once again my enemy. Miserable.

In those days many athletes experimented with specially mixed concoctions and energy replenishing foods in an attempt to stave off exhaustion, and it was common to find everything from guava jelly sandwiches to bananas stuffed into bike jerseys. My own "secret" in my first Ironman was to tape several sticks of black licorice to my top tube. By the end of the race they had melted onto the frame, but what did I know!

I was not used to being on the bike for 5 1/2 hours without touching the ground, and I had aches in my butt, my back, and my feet that I'd never known before. After the turn-around I was in 3rd place, with Dave Scott and Kim Bushong in front of me, riding behind the camera-trucks. I know they didn't plan it that way, but the vehicles gave them company and also blocked the wind for them. I would have appreciated having a truck too! It was disheartening to be out there alone, knowing there was no way I was going to catch the two leaders.

Everything in the Ironman leads up to the marathon. I got off the bike in fifth place, and started to run, but having been in the race now for about six and a half hours I was already exhausted, depleted and sore. Every aid station was like an oasis in the desert, and thankfully they were only a mile apart. I ran the race from one to the other, taking

. . . .

It's who you become as you overcome the obstacles necessary to achieve your goals, that can give you the deepest and most long lasting sense of fulfillment.
~ Anthony Robbins

. . . .

One often learns more from ten days of agony than from ten years of contentment.
~ Merle Shain

. . . .

One who gains strength by overcoming obstacles possesses the only strength which can overcome adversity.
~ Albert Schweitzer

. . . .

the time to grab a drink at each one, knowing that if I didn't I would most certainly run out of energy, or "bonk", as we say, somewhere on the run. During an endurance race like the Ironman you literally have to eat and drink your way through the event to maintain your energy level. It's a fine balance, though. Many well-trained athletes have wasted their effort on the lava fields of the King Kam because they either let themselves get dehydrated or they overloaded their stomachs.

Few people ever look good in this race, and after a while I figured out that I could tell how I was doing by people's reaction to me as I passed through the aid stations. At one point near the end of the marathon I remember staggering up to a group of volunteers at a water table only to see them physically shrink back as I approached. Finally one brave soul held out a cup of water and said, "Looking good!" I knew he was lying. By that time the muscles in my legs had cramped up so much that my thighs had become as hard as the pavement I was running on. I was hunched over, stiff as a robot, and every step was agony.

Strange things happen to the mind when the body is fatigued and stressed. I found that with all the blood and energy going to the muscles, my mind began to falter and play tricks on me. I began to lose concentration and couldn't think logically, and the simplest problems became conundrums. I remember trying to figure out how far I had to go once I reached 17 miles on the run, and I got to mile 18 without having solved the problem. Then, of course, I had to do the problem all over again.

Only coming into the town with the relief of the shade trees and the crowds lining the streets and cheering, did my head clear. I knew I was going to make it, and it was a wonderful feeling.

Over 90% of those who start the Hawaiian Ironman finish it, a surprisingly high number considering how tough the race is. Guts and pride are part of it, but there is something else too, an intangible quality about the race that perhaps only an Ironman finisher can understand. People have crawled across the finish line with bruised and aching bodies, totally exhausted, and yet still come back to do it all over again. Maybe it has to do with conquering fear and weakness, or proving oneself against the elements at an almost primitive level. Whatever it is, the Ironman provides the kind of challenge you rarely have to face in life.

I have to admit that the Ironman took me to the limit of my ability like nothing I had ever done before. I started out optimistically, believing that to finish the race in 91/2 hours was a realistic goal, and that certainly a top-ten finish was possible, but one by one I shed my expectations. In the end, the only goal left was the one that truly mattered: finishing the race. 11 hours and 4 minutes after the start of the race, I did just that.

I crossed the finish line with a mixture of emotions: disappointed to have slipped back to 47th place, and yet deeply satisfied that I had not given up. I shared a mental "high five" with my friend Frank, and hoped that wherever he was he was proud of me for achieving the goal we talked about so much.

It sounds corny to say that something inside me had changed forever, but that's how it felt. Physically crossing that line had made me an Ironman, and now when asked if I had done the race, I could say with resounding conviction, "Yes, I have". But mentally I had crossed a barrier, too. Along with my finisher's medal I took back to the mainland more confidence, more self-respect, and more strength to apply to my everyday life, and for me, that was the greatest reward.

By persisting, we achieve our goals, which gives us confidence, which in turn allows us to tackle other challenges. The more we do, the more we believe we can do, and that is what the circle of success is all about. *BL*

Chapter Two

Attitude

. . . .

Achieving goals by themselves will never make us happy in the long term; it's who you become as you overcome the obstacles necessary to achieve your goals, that can give you the deepest and most long lasting sense of fulfillment.
~ Anthony Robbins

. . . .

One of the illusions of life is that the present hour is not the critical, decisive hour. Write it on your heart that every day is the best day of the year.
~ Ralph Waldo Emerson

. . . .

This is the precious moment, but strangely, sadly, few people know it.
~ Timothy Ray Miller

. . . .

Enjoy the Process

*To finish the moment, to find the journey's end in every step of
the road, to live the greatest number of good hours, is wisdom.*
~ Ralph Waldo Emerson

There are probably few people who want to win as much as I do.
I've come to realize, however, that the process of preparing to win is
more significant in the long run than actually winning. The satisfaction of a win is short-lived, whereas the qualities we develop as we
work towards our goal of winning – discipline, persistence, and commitment – will last a lifetime. Too many of us forget to enjoy the journey.

As a young coach at U.C.I. in 1966 I began to realize that the
world of sports is a tough one, and that if my team didn't win, I'd be
out. So I wanted to win, badly. I had not won at the college level before, and to prove to the world and myself that I was one of the best
water polo coaches in America, I set my sights on winning the NCAA
Water Polo Championship in 1970. Winning became my driving force.
It's what got me up early and made me work long hours, trying to put
together a team that would be strong enough physically and mentally
to win. I led my players through endless drills and scrimmages, intense weight lifting sessions, lap after lap of swimming, and hours of
meetings. I spent five years living in the future, dreaming of winning
and working hard to that end.

Finally the big day came. We had made it to the finals, and were
pitted against UCLA. The team was coached by Bob Horn, who had
been named one of the Olympic coaches for the 1972 Games in Munich,
and to say we were rivals would be mild. Most of our confrontations
had been won by Horn, but I was confident the pendulum was about to
swing my way. I had a very talented team led by Ferdy Massimino, the

. . . .

A burning desire to be or do something gives us staying power - a reason to get up every morning or to pick ourselves up and start in again after a disappointment.
~ Marsha Sinetar

. . . .

If a man carefully examines his thoughts, he will be surprised to find how much he lives in the future. His well-being is always ahead.
~ Ralph Waldo Emerson

. . . .

He is blessed over all mortals who loses no moment of the passing life.
~ Henry David Thoreau

. . . .

Student Body President his senior year at U.C.I. He was a charismatic leader, and the guys had played together for several years and trusted each other to do their jobs. We were ready.

The game was close the whole way, but in the closing seconds Ferdy tossed in a lob shot to make the score 7-6, and that was it. We had won. After all this time I had finally achieved my goal, and I was elated. I went out to celebrate with my team, and the high lasted all night.

The next morning I woke up feeling flat. Empty. Like that beer can half empty on the counter, the fizz was gone. So soon? I was shocked. I don't know what I expected, but it wasn't this. I had thought that winning was the be-all and end-all of sports, and that if we won I would be carried through life on a wave of popularity and recognition. In reality, even those who knew about water polo didn't really care who had won or lost.

The following months were difficult ones. I sank into a depression and wandered around aimlessly, as did most of my players. I had reached my goal, but the victory proved less sweet than I expected. I did a lot of thinking and soul searching, and finally figured it out: winning is a hell of a lot better than losing, but what is most important is the process. Reaching a goal is nice, but true satisfaction comes from working towards that goal. It was probably the most important lesson of my coaching career. *EHN*

. . . .

Enthusiasm makes ordinary people
extraordinary.
~ Beverly Sills

. . . .

Don't worry about genius. Don't worry about
being clever. Trust to hard work,
perseverance, and determination. And the best
motto for a long march is: "Don't grumble.
Plug on!"
~ Sir Thomas Treves

. . . .

To different minds, the same world is hell,
and a heaven.
~ Ralph Waldo Emerson

. . . .

Enthusiasm Makes the Difference

*It's not doing the things we like, but by liking the things we do
that we can discover life's blessings.*
~ Goethe

When I was a young boy I had to work in the yard every Saturday morning to help my mother. I raked leaves, cut the lawn, and generally helped keep the area tidy. It was a drag. I would much rather have been playing ball or shooting hoops with my buddies. My mother used to tell me that since I had to do the job, I could look at it in two ways: I could dislike what I was doing and complain, or I could find ways to make the work enjoyable. It all depended on my attitude. Since I knew I had to do the work, I started thinking up ways to make it fun, like seeing how fast I could fill up a bag with leaves. To my surprise, I found that pretty soon the work was actually enjoyable.

Years later I was reminded of my mother's wisdom by one of the players on my team. Thomas Boughey was a long distance swimmer, and I started training him in the 1970's, just after the Munich Olympics had finished. At that time stories had begun to circulate about the training regimen of a couple of German athletes who had won gold medals. Their "secret" was to swim 25,000 yards a day, a tremendous distance even for a seasoned athlete. I was curious to see if Tommy could improve under this type of training, and he agreed to increase his workout to that distance. Swim goggles had just been invented, which made the job easier, but 25,000 yards is 14.2 miles, a long way however you want to look at it. (Nowadays swimmers do not cover such huge distances in training. They get fast by swimming 50, 100, and 200-yard repeats, but at 100% of effort. They also do a lot of work on stroke technique.)

I remember it used to take Tommy about six hours to swim the

. . . .

Life is 10% what you make of it, and 90%
how you take it.
~ *Irving Berlin*

. . . .

The master of the art of living makes little
distinction between his work and his play, his
labor and leisure, his mind and his body, his
education and recreation, his love and his
religion. He hardly knows which is which. He
simply pursues his vision of excellence in
whatever he does, leaving others to decide
whether he is working or playing. To him he is
always doing both. Never get so busy making a
living that you forget to make a life. Success
is best measured by how far you've come with
the talents you've been given. I can get up at
nine and be rested, or I can get up at
six and be President.
~ *Jimmy Carter*

. . . .

Your living is determined not so much by what
life brings to you as by the attitude you bring
to life; not so much by what happens to you as
by the way your mind looks at what happens.
~ *John Horner Miller*

. . . .

distance. I was impressed by his self-discipline, but what most amazed me was his unfailing attitude. Day after day he would appear to be enjoying the grueling hours in the pool. Often he would look up and make some ribald comment as I passed along the pool deck; he actually seemed to be having fun and was always laughing.

Tommy did improve a little, but not enough to warrant continuing the "experiment". He ended up winning several NCAA championships, but what I remember most about Tommy is his 100% positive attitude. I remember one day I asked him why he never complained, and his comment was: "When you know you have to do something, it is a lot more enjoyable to make it fun than to bitch and complain."

Almost what my mother would have said. *EHN*

. . . .

There's many a good tune played on an old fiddle.
~ *Samuel Butler*

. . . .

It's what you learn after you know it all that counts.
~ *John Wooden*

. . . .

It is a thousand times better to have common sense without education than to have education without common sense.
~ *Robert B. Ingersoll*

. . . .

Everything I Learned, My Mother Already Knew

Progress comes from the intelligent use of experience.
~ *Elbert Hubbard*

One of my fondest memories is of my mother in the kitchen, whistling happily as she prepared one of the many old family recipes she knew by heart. She loved to cook, and she was good at it, so we often had guests at our house. One thing I remember her saying is that she would never dream of trying out a new recipe the evening we had guests for dinner, just in case something went wrong. Sensible advice, as it turns out, even when applied to sport.

In 1982 I attempted my first significant triathlon challenge, the Hawaiian Ironman. A week before the race I decided to replace the seat on my bike with a lighter model, hoping to shave a few seconds off my time. When I sat on the new seat it seemed comfortable, and I thought I'd made an improvement. In the Ironman Triathlon most people spend between five and eight hours on the bike without getting off, so it is essential to have a comfortable seat. Many novice triathletes, however, are so desperate to get an edge on the competition that they sometimes abandon common sense in the hope of knocking a few seconds off their time. That was me! I thought the lighter saddle would make me go faster, and I ignored the fact that in an extended race, comfort is more important than weight.

By the time the bike leg ended my whole body was one giant cramp, and I ached like never before. It was all I could do to straighten up and start running stiffly along the road. I realized, too late, that I had spent nowhere near enough time in the saddle before the race to make sure it was comfortable. I should have stuck with my tried and trusted bike seat, just as my mother always served up a fail-safe recipe to our guests.

I had to learn the hard way never to experiment on the day of a race, either with a new piece of equipment, a new pair of shoes, or an untried sports drink. The moral of the story? Always, always, listen to your mother! *BL*

. . . .

*Success is the result of perfection, hard work,
learning from failure, loyalty, and persistence.*
~ Colin Powell

. . . .

*Almost any idea is good if a man has ability
and is willing to work hard. The best idea is
worthless if the creator is a loafer and
ineffective.*
~ William Feather

. . . .

*Nurture your minds with great thoughts. To
believe in the heroic makes heroes.*
~ Benjamin Disraeli

. . . .

Attitude is Everything

Who works achieves, and who sows reaps.
~ Arabian proverb

Over the years, I've come to rely on athletes who show me through their actions that they are reliable and willing to do what's necessary to make the team successful. Any talent that these players have I can develop, but give me a player with pounds of talent and no work ethic and I can do very little.

It doesn't take long to recognize who will work hard, who wants to improve, and who doesn't complain. One athlete who comes to mind is Scott Newcomb. I first met Scott in the late 1960's when he played on my summer club team, and as I got to know him I realized that he was determined to succeed in spite of his size. He did not have the strength and speed that come from being big, but he had a "fire-in-the-belly" kind of attitude that I can work with. In 1973 I invited Scott to attend a training camp at which the team for the World University Games in Moscow would be picked. Unfortunately, he did not play well during the camp, and I had a big decision to make: should I pass him over for someone who had shown more talent during the camp, or should I put my money on someone I knew I could rely on? Sometimes it takes a leap of faith, but rarely have I been disappointed when I have trusted my instincts. Scott was left-handed, an advantage in water polo, and agile, but more than that, I knew he was not afraid of hard work. He would persevere when the going got tough, his attitude had always been enthusiastic, and even though he had not played well during training, I trusted that I could rely on him once we got to the tournament.

My decision paid off. Scott went to the Games and proved himself a solid member of the team, and the team came away with a bronze

. . . .

*Go forward confidently, energetically
attacking problems, expecting
favorable outcomes.*
~ Norman Vincent Peale

. . . .

Attitudes are more important than facts.
~ Karl A. Menninger

. . . .

*Attitude is more important than the past, than
education, than money, than circumstances,
than what people do or say. It is more
important than appearance,
giftedness, or skill.*
~ Charles Swindoll

. . . .

medal for the United States. *EHN*

"For some reason, I did not play at all well during training camp that summer. Thankfully Newland knew what I was capable of and selected me for the team anyway. I believe that his decision was influenced by my attitude. Newland always taught us that talent isn't everything, that sometimes it's more important to have a good attitude and a willingness to work hard. I'm grateful that he trusted me and allowed me to enjoy the fruits of my efforts, and as I've built up a career in the real estate business I continue to realize the value of what he taught us. With the right attitude anyone can do anything they put their mind to, whether in business, sport, or family life.
    ~ Scott Newcomb*

Chapter Three

Focus

. . . .

The time your game is most vulnerable is when you're ahead. Never let up.
~ Rod Laver

. . . .

Everybody pulls for David, nobody roots for Goliath.
~ Wilt Chamberlain

. . . .

Racing is a matter of spirit, not strength.
~ Janet Guthrie

. . . .

Don't Stop When You Get to the Top

Becoming number one is easier than staying number one.
~ Senator Bill Bradley

In sports and politics alike you need to be focused, intense, and committed to your goal in order to get to the top. What many people don't realize is that you need those same qualities to stay there.

In the summer of 1967 my team went to Chicago for the AAU Water Polo National Championships. We returned home with the first place trophy and a new air of confidence. We had held our own against the best players in the country, and had reached a higher level of play. The local paper ran a full-page photo of our team holding the trophy, and a lengthy article about Newland and the team winning its first national championship. We were feeling pretty good about ourselves.

Most of us were lifeguards for Newport Beach, and we had been playing in a league throughout the summer. About a week after our return from Chicago we were scheduled to play our final game, against our arch rival, the Huntington Beach Lifeguard Department. As newly crowned national champions, we were totally unconcerned about the outcome. On the evening of the game, some of our team didn't bother to show up, and some sauntered in late. Our warm-up was half-hearted, for we knew we would win. After all, we were the champions.

The Huntington Beach team was fired up. They had seen the article about us in the newspaper and knew we had won the Nationals, and they played with the focus of a lion in the hunt. By half time, our championship team was down by several goals, and although Newland did his best to get our heads back into the game, it was too late. Once you've lost your focus, it's hard to find it under that type of stress. We

. . . .

You find that you have peace of mind and can enjoy yourself, get more sleep and rest when you know that it was a one hundred percent effort that you gave – win or lose.
~ Gordie Howe

. . . .

When you step onto that field, you cannot concede a thing.
~ Gayle Sayers

. . . .

It's amazing how much of this is mental. Everybody's in good shape. Everybody knows how to ski. Everybody has good equipment. When it really boils down to it, it's who wants it the most, and who's the most confident on his skis.
~ Reggie Crist

. . . .

ended up losing to a team of guys who played harder than we did, and who wanted to prove a point. They were jubilant at having beaten the national champions; for us it was a lesson in humility.

Our arrogance had tarnished the trophy we had been so proud to win, and the fact that it was the last game of the summer only made it worse. We now had to live with the knowledge that we had let each other down and bitterly disappointed Newland in the process. Within days we each received a hand-written letter from Newland, spelling out his frustration at our performance. He had known before the game started that we were in trouble. He made it very clear that part of being a champion involves being prepared to play every game as hard as you can, especially once you reach the top, where everyone is out to knock you down. He said that being a champion means never taking strength for granted, never under-estimating the competition, and always, always, always staying focused. Thirty-four years later, the lesson is still fresh in my mind. *BL*

. . . .

One day Alice came to a fork in the road and saw a Cheshire cat in a tree. "Which road do I take?" she asked. "Where do you want to go?" was his response. "I don't know," Alice answered. "Then", said the cat, "It doesn't matter".
~ *Lewis Carroll*

. . . .

Self-respect is the root of discipline; the sense of dignity grows with the ability to say no to oneself.
~ *Abraham J. Heschel*

. . . .

If you don't know where you're going, you might wind up someplace else.
~ *Yogi Berra*

. . . .

"Jack of All Trades, Master of None"

*It is better to excel in any single art than to arrive only
at mediocrity in several.*
~ Pliny the Younger

We all need someone in our lives to keep us on the right track.
Sometimes that person is a parent, sometimes it's an honest friend, or
if you are an athlete, sometimes it's your coach. It's best to take their
advice.

One summer, between my junior and senior years of water polo, I
got into the habit of playing volleyball at the UCI gym with my best
friend, Randy Howatt. Maybe I was bored with the routine of water
polo, or simply lacked the necessary degree of discipline to concentrate on one thing, but whatever my excuse, I should have known better. At 5'9" and limited to about a six-inch vertical jump, I was not on
the "most talented player" list for volleyball. Water polo was where
my talent lay, and it was paying my way through college in the form of
a scholarship. I should have respected that, and committed myself to
improving in water polo, but at the time it seemed more fun to play
volleyball.

One evening we were in the gym as usual, practicing setting and
"spiking" the ball over the net. Out of the corner of my eye I noticed
the door open and a figure step into the gym. He stood just inside the
doorway, silhouetted against the evening sky, and even with his fea-
tures in darkness I knew it was Newland. My heart sank. He didn't say
a word, just watched for a minute or two, then turned abruptly and
walked out.

With a sense of guilt I remembered Newland telling us over and
over again that we needed to focus on what we were good at, and forget the rest. In his inimitable way he used to say that the more you try

. . . .

Often, he who does too much, does too little.
~ *Italian Proverb*

. . . .

A person with half volition goes backwards and forwards, but makes no progress on even the smoothest of roads.
~ *Thomas Carlyle*

. . . .

Determine what specific goal you want to achieve. Then dedicate yourself to its attainment with a total singleness of purpose, the trenchant zeal of a crusader.
~ *Paul J. Myer*

. . . .

to do, the more you half-ass everything, and the harder it is to achieve anything. I had heard this from him so many times, reiterated in so many ways, that just his presence in the gym that evening spoke volumes. To him the choice was simple: I could be an All American, maybe even go to the Olympics in water polo, or I could, at best, be a mediocre volleyball player. It was up to me.

His unspoken disapproval stung. I realized I had lost my focus, and that playing volleyball would do nothing to improve my water polo skills. I knew what I had to do. The next day I was back in the pool, and I didn't play volleyball again until the end of my senior year in college.

Newland was right: when we focus on what we're good at, we are often rewarded with success. That year I made All American, was named Player of the All U.C. Tournament in Santa Barbara, and Most Valuable Player of our water polo team.

Sometimes we have to choose between what is fun and what is right. If we're lucky enough to have someone in our life to point us in the right direction, we should listen to them. Although it was a blast playing volleyball with Randy, Newland made me realize that I had to honor my commitment to water polo. And I'm glad I did, because while I can be proud of my athletic achievements in water polo, to this day I can't "spike" a volleyball over the net. *BL*

. . . .

Enter every activity without giving mental recognition to the possibility of defeat. Concentrate on your strengths, instead of your weaknesses...on your powers, instead of your problems.
~ *Paul J Meyer*

. . . .

From a certain point onward there is no longer any turning back. That is the point that must be reached.
~ *Franz Kafka*

. . . .

It takes courage to push yourself to places you have never been before...to test your limits...to break through barriers. And the day came when the risk it took to remain tight inside the bud was more painful than the risk it took to blossom.
~ *Anais Nin*

. . . .

Get a Grip on Fear

Anything I've ever done that ultimately was worthwhile...initially scared me to death.
~ Betty Bender

The sport of kayaking is an unusual one in that there are no officially recorded world records. Conditions are too variable: headwinds, tailwinds, currents, and the advantages or disadvantages of different lanes mean that you can race the course fifty times and never have the same result. Anything can happen, and that was the problem. There I was in May of 1974, about to compete in the finals of the National Kayak Team trials in Ohio, and beginning to question myself. Had I done enough? Were other people in better shape? Was I rested and ready to give my best? I was headed into the unknown, and nerves were taking over.

At some point, usually right before a race, every competitor questions his or her ability. When you are out there training, there is no pressure of competition and you are mentally comfortable, knowing there is still time to prepare. On the day of the race, however, judgment is imminent. No more time to work out or fine-tune your performance, only the race to contemplate. It is normal to feel those "butterflies", but to be successful you have to get them flying in formation.

I'd learned, playing water polo for Newland, that the outcome of a game was determined in the hours before it. If we were goofing around in the pool, throwing the ball to each other and laughing, it seemed that we always performed poorly. Rather than getting psyched up, which is what we thought we were doing, we were actually losing focus. If I gave myself some time alone to think, I usually performed better.

This was a "make or break" event for me, and I knew it. From the K-1 single kayak event I was about to take part in, the national team would be selected, an important step in going to the 1976 Montreal

. . . .

Once you're physically capable of winning a gold medal, the rest is 90% mental.
~ *Patti Johnson*

. . . .

If you want to take your mission in life to the next level, if you're stuck and you don't know how to rise, don't look outside yourself. Look inside. Don't let your fears keep you mired in the crowd. Abolish your fears and raise your commitment level to the point of no return, and I guarantee you that the Champion Within will burst forth to propel you toward victory.
~ *Bruce Jenner*

. . . .

Panic is a sudden desertion of us, and a going over to the enemy of our imagination.
~ *Christian Nevell Bovee*

. . . .

Olympics. My goal was finally in sight, but I felt an incredible pressure to perform. I had made so many sacrifices and dedicated so much time to this sport, that if the race didn't go as I hoped, I'd have to rethink my goal. Doubts about my ability began to weigh me down and I felt defeated even before the start of the race. Knowing that this mind-set could lead to a disastrous result only made the situation worse.

Standing on the side of that lake in Ohio, I knew that if I were to have any chance of restoring my confidence, I had to be by myself and give myself a little pep-talk. I left the other athletes talking and joking on the beach, and paddled my kayak slowly across the lake. In the early morning the water was smooth as glass, and I glided to the middle of the lake, used the paddle to balance my boat, and began to think.

At this level everyone is extremely fit, and since the time between first and last place would only be about 2 seconds, it occurred to me that those two seconds would be mostly mental. Instead of letting my thoughts wander fearfully into the future, worrying about how I'd do, I realized I should simply paddle my own race and focus on doing my best. Even if I didn't do well, at least I'd walk away with my self-respect intact, which along with our health is the most precious thing we possess. I felt fit, had trained hard, and I deserved to be there. I should try to live in the moment, instead of fearing the future.

On the quiet of the lake I let these thoughts wash over me, and soon I began to feel a new energy. The decision to focus on my own race and not worry about other people seemed to lift a burden from my shoulders, and after a few sprints to warm up, I paddled to the start of the race with a fresh confidence.

It turned out to be the best race I ever had in a singles boat. About 100 meters from the finish I found a burst of power and was able to finish as strong as I had started, winning by 1 1/2 seconds. Although I had won numerous singles events over the years, this was the only significant race I ever won in the 500 meters against the best athletes in the U.S.

Twenty-seven years later I realize that however satisfied I was at making the national team, the most significant achievement that day was handling my fear out there on the water, before the race had even started. We must never be reluctant to put ourselves into a situation in which we are afraid, for whether our challenge is a race, or a presentation at work, or overcoming a phobia, the one thing we need to practice is how to overcome our fear. The more we do it, the easier it gets, and the stronger we will be. *BL*

. . . .

*If you have to remind yourself to concentrate
during competition, you've got no
chance to concentrate.*
~ Bobby Nichols

. . . .

*Concentration is why some athletes are better
than others. You develop that concentration in
training. You can't be lackluster in training
and concentrate in a meet.*
~ Edwin Moses

. . . .

*Every situation presents us with an
opportunity to automatically react or
consciously respond: a choice point...We
are a product of our choices, not of our
circumstances.*
~ Eric Allenbaugh

. . . .

A Delicate Balance

You have to block everything out and be extremely focused, and be
relaxed and mellow too.
~ Jennifer Capriati

When I went to the Olympics in 1976, I thought it would be easy to give a peak performance. My kayak partner, Mike Johnson, and I had trained so hard, through setbacks and injuries and in my case the break-up of my first marriage, that once we had qualified I thought the rest would be plain sailing. After all, I would be at a gathering of the world's best athletes where the focus would surely be on sport, so all we had to do was give the kind of performance we had at the Olympic Trials and we'd be taking home a medal. How wrong I was! It was a delicate balance, wanting to fully experience this phenomenal world event, yet having to prepare for my race. The pressure was impossible to imagine, and I realized that to be successful in any athletic event away from home, it's important to learn to focus.

We were in Montreal with 5,500 athletes from almost 150 countries, crowded into an area the size of a small town. A babble of different languages surrounded us as we tried to find our way around. Security was intense because of the nightmare of the Munich Olympics four years earlier, in which a Palestinian terrorist attack resulted in the death of 11 Israeli athletes. Two soldiers with machine guns accompanied each bus that took us to the racecourse, and every day we took a different route to prevent terrorists from planning an attack. We had to wear special identification tags wherever we went, and a 20 ft high fence of barbed wire surrounded the village. I tried not to waste mental energy on the nagging fear that the Munich incident could be repeated, but it was difficult not to be a little distracted.

Joe Bottom, one of America's best swimmers in the 1976 Olym-

. . . .

Concentration is the ability to think about absolutely nothing when it is absolutely necessary.
~ *Ray Knight*

. . . .

You can not always control what goes on outside. But you can always control what goes on inside.
~ *Wayne Dyer*

. . . .

If you focus on results you will never change. If you focus on change, you will get results.
~ *Jack Dixon*

. . . .

pics, told me that his coach, Mark Schubert, had given him a simple guideline to follow: the athletes who would win the medals would be those who rested and slept the most. It was hard to follow his advice, however. The Olympics is a chance for athletes to mingle and get to know each other, and there were parties, concerts, and dances late into the night. My wife Julie qualified for the team a week after I did, and although we were married, she had to stay in the women's building. The gymnasts she shared a room with finished their competition during the first week of the Games, so for them it was time to party. The challenge for us kayakers was to keep our focus on competing. Athletes like Joe set an example for us all: not only did he resist the temptation to party, he also gave up the honor and excitement of marching in the Opening Ceremonies in order to stay off his feet and out of the sun, resting for his event. Since he won a gold medal, it's hard to argue with the philosophy.

Just walking down the street there were distractions. Other athletes bombarded me with offers to trade pins, those small and very collectible ceramic or metal badges given to us by our Olympic Committees or the sponsors of the Games. In my office at home I have a cap studded with pins, and although I'm glad to have it as a memento, the trading distracted me from our real purpose for being there. I was also stopped every few yards by someone who wanted my autograph, and eventually I grew so tired of explaining who I was, what I did, and what exactly kayaking was, that I began to sign the name Bruce Jenner to stop the questions. Everyone knew the popular decathlete, and there are now a lot of people out there with fake Bruce Jenner autographs. Years later I told Bruce what I'd done, and he laughed pretty hard.

As athletes we had access to almost all the sporting events. It was tempting to watch as much of the track and field and swimming competitions as possible, but I had to keep reminding myself that I was not there as a spectator and I should be focusing on training and peaking for my own races.

Mike and I knew that in our first race we had little chance of qualifying for the semi-finals, so we decided to save our energy for the repechage, a series of races in which eliminated contestants have another chance to move to the next round. The race was set up in such a way that whoever came second would be in the easiest semi-final the next day, and that's what we were aiming for. Unfortunately, so were all the other teams in the race, and with everyone trying to hold out for second place, the result was a photo finish. Mike and I ended up fourth, which meant we completely missed any chance of advancing to the semis.

I was very disappointed, but not disheartened, for just to be at the Olympic Games was an honor. Next time I would do things differently, but I realized how rare it is to possess both the talent and the focus to excel in a competition like the Olympics. It's a delicate balance, and those who have achieved it are the supreme athletes of our time. They deserve every one of their medals. *BL*

Chapter Four

Self-Discipline

. . . .

*Brave is the lion tamer, brave is the world
subduer, but braver is the one who has
subdued himself.*
~ *Johann Gottfried Von Herder*

. . . .

*Nothing gives a person so much advantage
over another as to remain always cool and
unruffled in all circumstances.*
~ *Thomas Jefferson*

. . . .

*He who reigns within himself and rules
passions, desires, and fears is more than a
king.*
~ *John Milton*

. . . .

Cool at the Pool

*If you are patient in one moment of anger, you will escape
a hundred days of sorrow.*

~ Chinese proverb

George Orwell once wrote, "Serious sport has nothing to do with fair play. It is bound up with hatred, jealousy, boastfulness, disregard of all rules and sadistic pleasure in witnessing violence: in other words it is war minus the shooting." There is certainly a visible lack of self-discipline in professional sports these days, and my only explanation is that it sells. Management and coaches must believe that vulgar language and fights are what the fans want to see, and that this display of unrestrained aggression will increase the number of people who come to the arena or watch a game on T.V. However, it's not the way to go. Anger and other negative emotions are a distraction; they take the mind out of the present, where it must be to perform well, and put it in the past. This is always counterproductive. Time and time again I've noticed that when a player loses control, his performance goes down the tubes. I've learned that if I want my players to perform well, I must teach them to control their emotions, but to do so I had to learn control myself.

Like a lot of coaches, I used to yell and scream and let my emotions get too heated. I can't tell you how many times I have gotten angry at my failure to get a team to perform as I would like them to, and then transferred this anger to the referee, blaming him rather than myself for the problem. I had to learn control the hard way: by coming so close to losing it that I scared myself.

The incident that shook me to my senses happened in 1961, during a game against Garden Grove High School. Ron Degler, considered

. . . .

No one can make you jealous, angry,
vengeful, or greedy – unless you let them.
~ *Napoleon Hill*

. . . .

The world belongs to the enthusiast who keeps
his cool.
~ *William McFee*

. . . .

I count him braver who overcomes his desires
than him who conquers his enemies; for the
hardest victory is the victory over self.
~ *Aristotle*

. . . .

one of the best officials in the area, was the referee. We were losing, and there had been some close calls that went against us. Just before the end of the game, Spencer Richardson, our hole-man, fired a backhand that skipped under the goalie's arm and appeared to float into the cage for a goal. This would have tied the game, but Degler disputed the goal and did not allow it. I was seething.

When the game was over, I walked down the pool deck and around to where Degler stood and grabbed him by the shirt, lifting him off the ground with one hand. I was about to hammer him against the wall with the other hand when at the last minute I came to my senses. "What the hell am I doing?" I thought. I realized just how far I had gone over the line, and my lack of self-control shocked me. My actions could have damaged both his health and my career, and I knew at that moment what my limits needed to be.

I bet that 95% of the anger directed at sports officials by players and coaches starts with self-anger. Many players and coaches never figure this out, because they don't take the time to really understand themselves. When I'm coaching a game these days I rarely get out of my chair, and some people think I'm detached and aloof. Actually, I've learned to keep my emotions tightly under control. I'm totally absorbed in what's happening, but I'm always in the present or in the future, never dwelling on a call that's gone against my team or a shot that should have scored. If I'm thinking of something that's already happened that I cannot change, I'm not much help to my team. I've learned that I can be a more effective coach by controlling my emotions and modeling self-restraint. I'm sure the referees appreciate it too. *EHN*

. . . .

Discipline is the soul of an army. It makes small numbers formidable; procures success to the weak, and esteem to all.
~ *George Washington*

. . . .

What we do upon some great occasion will probably depend on what we already are. What we are will be the result of previous years of self-discipline.
~ *Henry Parry Liddon*

. . . .

He who lives without discipline dies without honor.
~ *Icelandic proverb*

. . . .

"Hell Week"

We must all suffer from one of two pains: the pain of discipline or the pain of regret. The difference is discipline weighs ounces, while regret weighs tons.
~ *Jim Rohn*

One of the best players I've ever had at UCI was Mike Evans, and he ended up playing on three U.S. Olympic teams. When he came to train with me the summer before his freshman year, he was only 18 years old and the Olympics were still just a dream for him. Physically he was intimidating, and his strength was awesome, and as we hammered away at workouts over the next two months his effort impressed me. We would work out twice a day: 1½ hours in the weight room in the morning, followed by 2 hours in the pool, then in the evening we'd spend 3 more hours in the pool. It was intense, but he stuck with it.

Being new to the program, we hadn't talked much, but about two weeks before the start of the season he came up to me at workout one afternoon with a look of apprehension on his face. He asked me when "Hell Week" was going to start; he knew that other schools were beginning their practices and that "Hell Week" was a traditional rite of passage. He was beginning to worry.

"Hell Week" is a week or two of extra-hard workouts intended to get the players into shape. It is accompanied by aches and pains and near exhaustion from an excruciating schedule that the athletes aren't used to. I could tell Mike was nervous talking to me, afraid of what my answer was going to be. He had been pushing himself for the past few months, and the thought of putting in even more effort had gotten to him. He was surprised and very relieved when I said:

"I don't believe in "Hell Week". Players should be in shape all the

. . . .

The key to life is accepting challenges. Once someone stops doing this, he is dead.
~ *Bette Davis*

. . . .

The only discipline that lasts is self-discipline.
~ *Bum Phillips*

. . . .

Lack of discipline leads to frustration and self-loathing.
~ *Marie Chapian*

. . . .

time. "Hell Week" is only for those who do not have the self-discipline and motivation to stay in shape all year long. We're different; we pay our dues every single day. If we stay in shape, then we'll never need to experience the pain of getting back into good physical condition. I stay in shape, and I expect you to do the same". *EHN*

With Newland we saw first hand what it meant to be self-disciplined, and passionate about it. He was a positive role model for all of us, and I have never forgotten the conversation I had with him about "Hell Week". Even now, years later, I am motivated to "pay my dues" every day to stay in shape.
~Mike Evans, U.C.I. Water Polo 1978-80

. . . .

Most true happiness comes from one's inner life, from the disposition of the mind and soul. Admittedly, a good inner life is difficult to achieve, especially in these trying times. It takes reflection and contemplation and self-discipline.
~ *W.L. Shirer*

. . . .

Without discipline, there is no life at all.
~ *Katherine Hepburn*

. . . .

One can have no smaller or greater mastery than mastery of oneself.
~ *Leonardo da Vinci*

. . . .

The First Step is the Hardest

There is no such thing as a great talent without great willpower.
~ Honore de Balzac

I have always said there is no secret to success, only self-discipline and hard work. When my alarm goes off at 3:50 each morning I grope to shut it off and then put my feet on the floor before I can give in to my excuses. Getting out of bed is tough, but I do it. I know how easy it would be to simply lay back down, but there's never any question in my mind about going back to sleep. I've found that the earlier I get up and the harder I work, the more positive my attitude is about my ability to coach and win. As I drive to workout in the morning and see all the homes in darkness, I get great satisfaction from knowing that I am tougher mentally and emotionally than all those people who are still asleep.

That's how I want my players to feel. I want them to know when they get to a tournament that they are tougher than the competition, that they have lifted more weights, done more legwork, and shot more balls. That they have practiced when others have not, worked out and eaten breakfast before others were even out of bed. It takes self-discipline, but the reward is confidence, and it will give them the edge every time. They may, in the end, get beaten, but they will know they haven't been out-worked.

My philosophy is simple and my players know it: work harder than the other guy, and you will probably beat him. *EHN*

The effort needed to gain Newland's respect was seemingly impossible, but it gave us a tremendous drive to succeed and accomplish the goal. If you were "one of his guys", you simply practiced enor-

. . . .

Chase your passion, not your pension.
~ *Denis Waitley*

. . . .

The feeling of being valuable—"I am a valuable person"—is essential to mental health and is a cornerstone of self-discipline...because when one considers oneself valuable one will take care of oneself in all ways that are necessary.
Self-discipline is self-caring.
~ *M. Scott Peck*

. . . .

We could hardly wait to get up in the morning.
~ *Wilbur Wright*

. . . .

mous personal discipline or you did not survive in Newland's world. This included swimming and water polo workouts that were ahead of their time in terms of difficulty and challenge. If we doubted ourselves, Newland was always there to provide inspiration that was personal, sincere, and unique in its ability to drive us even further. Ultimately, however, it was up to us to find the self-discipline to succeed.

My friends and associates often ask how, at the age of 56, I have the discipline to work out every day. I know, without question, that the influence of Newland has inspired a commitment that will last a lifetime. It has had a direct application upon my personal and business life, for in difficult times it is enormously helpful to call upon good habits to help you through seemingly impossible challenges. I consider the self-discipline I learned from Newland a lifetime gift.

~ Randy Howatt, U.C.I Water Polo 1965-66

. . . .

Expect trouble as an inevitable part of life and repeat to yourself the most comforting words of all: "This, too, shall pass."
~ Ann Landers

. . . .

People are like stained glass windows. They sparkle and shine when the sun is out, but when the darkness sets in, their true beauty is revealed only if there is a light from within.
~ Elizabeth Kubler Ross

. . . .

He is happy whose circumstances suit his temper; but he is more excellent who suits his temper to any circumstances.
~ David Hume

. . . .

Expect the Unexpected

Man is an animal who more than any other can adapt himself to all climates and circumstances.
~ Henry David Thoreau

What makes us tough? Facing a situation and finding a solution. Learning to be adaptable and innovative when things don't go our way. Persisting. Years of competing in over a thousand events have taught me that what I least expect to happen probably will, and that when it does, I need to focus on my goal and stay with it. I've crashed my bike during races, missed turns, lost water bottles, and had such bad leg cramps that it was like running on stilts. Once I even went off course, and swam across a stream that had alligators in it. Luckily I'm still around to say that although we can't always control what happens, we can control our reaction to what happens, and that's how we become tough.

The most unpredictable aspect in any race is the weather. Every race director fears that inclement conditions will ruin an event, because while you can control the timing of a race, the advertising and the volunteers, you have no say in the weather. The annual triathlon in Wilkes-Barre, Pennsylvania was a case in point. As a tribute to the flawless organization of the race director, Jerry Kowalski, and her staff, the race was selected as the 1988 Olympic Distance Triathlon National Championship race (1500m swim, 40km bike, & 10km run). A supremely challenging course combined with stellar organization, hospitality, and community support made this a jewel of a race, and I was looking forward to it. The day before the race I drove the course to familiarize myself with the steep climbs and sharp turns of the route.

. . . .

Life is a grindstone. But whether it grinds us down or polishes us up depends on us.
~ *L. Thomas Holdcroft*

. . . .

Practice easing your way along. Don't get het up or in a dither. Do your best; take it as it comes. You can handle anything if you think you can. Just keep your cool and your sense of humor.
~ *Smiley Blanton, MD*

. . . .

And when it rains on your parade, look up rather than down. Without the rain, there would be no rainbow.
~ *Jerry Chin*

. . . .

The weather was calm and sunny, perfect for a race.

Who could have predicted that overnight a huge storm would blow in? I awoke at 4:30am to the sound of pounding rain, and when I got up, the sky seemed to have collapsed. Four inches of rain were dumped on us that day; the road was slick, the curves treacherous; the conditions were the worst I'd ever raced in. However, you do what you have to do, and I made it through the bike course without crashing. When I got off my bike, my feet were so numb with cold I could hardly run. The thought crossed my mind that it would be much easier to give up than to stay in the race, but as I headed into the wind to complete the run, I knew I'd only be giving up my self-respect. While I could still run, I would not quit.

As the race came to an end, athletes wandered in all directions, chilled to the bone and looking for shelter from the freezing rain. The refreshment and medical tent area began to look like a battlefield casualty ward. The race committee responded admirably to the unexpected conditions by borrowing piles of white blankets from a local hospital. The whole scene became surreal. Hundreds of ashen, dripping bodies swathed in white stood ankle-deep in mud, looking out over the lush green hills that two hundred and fifty years before had echoed with the sound of muskets in skirmishes with the Connecticut Indians. The only battle being waged today was against the elements, but for those of us in the fight, it was a tough one.

When we are faced with an unexpectedly difficult situation, we either refuse to give up, and adapt as best we can, or we shrink from the challenge. When we refuse to give up, we get stronger. Although I won the Masters (over 40) division that day, the true winners were all the athletes who finished the race. Almost as a tribute to their persistence, the sun broke through the storm clouds, and as the last competitors straggled across the finish line, a brilliant rainbow arched across the sky. *BL*

Chapter Five

Commitment

· ·

The road to happiness lies in two simple
principles: find what it is that interests you
and that you can do well, and when you find it
put your whole soul into it — every bit of
energy and ambition and natural
ability you have.
~ *John D. Rockefeller III*

· · · · · · · · · · · · · ·

Be an all-out, not a hold-out.
~ *Norman Vincent Peale*

· · · · · · · · · · · · · ·

Without involvement, there is no commitment.
Mark it down, asterisk it, circle it, underline it:
No involvement, no commitment.
~ *Stephen Covey*

· ·

Vote with Your Feet

*Losers make promises they often break. Winners make
commitments they always keep.*
~ Denis Waitley

I truly believe that commitment is 90% of success. Every day, from the moment we get up, we show what is important to us by how we choose to spend our time. When we fail to show up at workout, school, or a job, or we show up late, what we're really saying is that we are not committed enough to make the effort to be there. Many of my players make the excuse that they missed practice because they had to study or finish a paper that they only just found out about. We all know that the real reason was that either they didn't spend their time effectively and weren't in class when they should have been, or they wasted their time socializing and playing hanky panky with some lady. They can try justifying their actions, but the only thing that really counts is what they did and how they elected to spend their time. That, to me, is the bottom line.

I once had a player who always showed up, right from the start. Jim Kruse was strong, intense, and had great concentration; it didn't take me long to figure out he was going to have a big impact on my program. He played for me from 1972-'73, and would score more last minute goals to win games than any player I've ever had. He was always on the ball (he thought the best defense was to outscore the other team) and in on the action. He loved the pressure. Kruse was consistent, dependable, knew what he wanted, but what is most important, he was always there to get it. The kind of player I love to have on my team. *EHN*

I thought I could never go to UCI. In high school I had read ar-

. . . .

*Those who attain any excellence commonly
spend life in one pursuit, for excellence is not
often granted upon easier terms.*
~ *Samuel Johnson*

. . . .

*The first thing is to love your sport. Never do it
to please someone else. It has to be yours.*
~ *Peggy Fleming*

. . . .

*The quality of a person's life is in direct
proportion to their commitment to excellence,
regardless of their chosen field of endeavor.*
~ *Vince Lombardi*

. . . .

ticles in the *LA Times Sports Section* about the UCI water polo players, and the image portrayed was that all Newland's guys were in the weight room by 5:30am, could bench press 325 pounds, and could swim a 100 yards freestyle in 48 seconds flat. I was intimidated.

Then it came, a barely legible 3x5 card in a hand-written envelope: "Come and work out with us". Newland wanted to recruit me! The unthinkable happened: I, Jim Kruse, went to a UCI spring workout. And survived. Newland said hello to me, and what's more, I wanted to go back.

When I walked into the next workout he said, "How's it going, kid?" It was going well, very well. This time I got to scrimmage a lot, and I am talking about scrimmaging with NCAA Champions and US National team players. I was never going to leave this.

At my third workout, I found that guys he was also speaking to about attending UCI were not there. WERE NOT THERE! They missed that workout; I did not. Newland noticed.

I came back on the fourth day. I found out that not everyone benched a Volkswagon, nor did they all swim like Olympic medallists (although we did have some in the program). At last it seemed within my grasp. Then a defining moment in my athletic career occurred: I played with "UCI guys" in a spring AAU tournament, and played a lot. It was an insignificant tournament, but I was playing with former CIF champions, NCAA champions, US National team players, and most important of all, I was playing for Newland. I would never turn back.

~ *Jim Kruse, U.C.I. Water Polo 1972-73*

. . . .

You've touched people and know it. You've touched people and never may know it. Either way, no matter what your life feels like to you right now, you have something to give. It is in giving to one another that each one of our lives becomes meaningful.

~ *Laura Schlessinger*

. . . .

The man born with a talent which he was meant to use finds his greatest happiness in using it.

~ *Johann Wolfgang von Goethe*

. . . .

Our prayers are answered not when we are given what we ask, but when we are challenged to be what we can be.

~ *Morris Adler*

. . . .

Coach Like You Think They're Listening (Sometimes They Are)

We cannot live only for ourselves. A thousand fibers connect us with our fellow-men; and along those fibers, as sympathetic threads, our actions run as causes, and they come back to us as effects.
~ Herman Melville

Sometimes when I'm coaching I feel like I'm just out there shouting into the wind; my words seem to zip right over the heads of the kids in the water and ricochet back off the pool deck. It frustrates me, but I don't give up. It is my duty to throw out the best I have, and hope that some of what I believe in so passionately will hit the mark. I've learned from many years of coaching that some of it does, mainly because of a player I had named Jeff Harvey.

I recruited Jeff in 1987. He was large and very fast, and he was on the 1989 team that won the NCAA Championships, although he did not play in any of the games. For some reason Jeff never reached the level I thought he would, and I didn't think he was getting much out of what I was saying. It has always been hard for me to accept that some kids have great talent but lack the discipline to develop it, and when he ended up drifting away from the program I wrote him off as one of the ones I "lost". How wrong I was.

One day I ran into Jeff at the Corona del Mar pool. He wore a bright red bandana around his head and gave me the grim news he'd been diagnosed with testicular cancer. The chemotherapy had made all his hair fall out. I was surprised at the determination in his voice when he told me he was swimming again to get back into shape, that he'd quit drinking and staying out late, and he was eating better. He

. . . .

True happiness...is not attained through self-gratification, but through fidelity to a worthy purpose.
~ *Helen Keller*

. . . .

Our grand business in life is not to see what lies dimly at a distance, but to do what clearly lies at hand.
~ *Thomas Carlyle*

. . . .

No one's death comes to pass without making some impression, and those close to the deceased inherit part of the liberated soul and become richer in their humanness.
~ *Herman Broch*

. . . .

said that playing water polo at UCI had taught him how to fight to win, and he would never give up battling this disease. For the first time in his life he felt that he was taking control.

I was blown away. All the years he played on my team, and I never thought he was listening as I hammered away about the importance of self-discipline and strength of character. I was stunned to realize that in fact Jeff probably took in more of what I was trying to teach than many of the star players on the team.

He started coming over to my house quite regularly to talk, and I saw that his days in the water polo program had planted in him the seeds of a tremendously positive attitude. Now, just when he needed it the most, he was reaping the harvest.

It would be a great story if Jeff had won the fight, but he didn't. He died in 1996, only 28 years old.

I have done a lot of thinking since those final talks with Jeff. I'm glad that right until the end he was able to live a positive life, drawing inspiration from the structure and discipline he remembered from his water polo days. By fighting so hard when his life was on the line, he taught me never to compromise on coaching with passion, because we never know who we are going to affect. Jeff was listening, and when it came down to it, he proved himself a winner in the deepest sense of the word. *EHN*

Jeff was a senior when I was a redshirt freshman. He seemed bitter about everything and he and Newland gave each other a pretty hard time, so when he came down with terminal cancer a few years later I was amazed to learn that the thing he held onto most in that difficult time was his experience playing water polo at U.C.I. He gave whatever money he could to the Newport Water Polo Foundation and spent time visiting Newland and talking to him. It seemed to give him strength.

~ Peter Muller, U.C.I. Water Polo 1991-95

. . . .

My greatest point is my persistence. I never give up in a match.
~ Bjorn Borg

. . . .

Never give up. Keep your thoughts and mind always on the goal.
~ Tom Bradley

. . . .

I am a slow walker, but I never walk backwards.
~ Abraham Lincoln

. . . .

Walk the straight line to your goal

The butterfly becomes only when it's entirely ready.
~ Chinese proverb

Water polo is one of the hardest sports to learn because the skills required are so different than any other sport. Unless you have played in one of the few age group programs, by the time you start playing you are usually 14 or 15 years old. You have already learned how to catch and throw a ball, but not in water. Catching and throwing a ball with one hand while treading water is a difficult skill, and it takes years to master. Learning patience has always been a very important part of my program.

Many of the players I get from high school programs do not have the technical skills to play water polo at the college level, so I have to "red-shirt" a lot of them, which means they can practice with the team, but they don't play in games. This preserves their eligibility for an additional year, giving them a chance to learn the system and improve their skills. It also gives them another year to mature, both physically and emotionally. The delay can be tough, though. It is hard to be on the fringes when you are young and longing to be in on the action. If a player can't hang in there and work hard for the sheer joy of playing, he will never make it in my program. Many don't have the patience, and they quit or transfer to another school. Some of them, however, show great self-discipline, and learn delayed gratification. They are the ones who succeed. One of the things I like most about coaching at UCI is that almost every year someone unexpected emerges to play a major role in the success of the team. John Redd was a case in point.

John came to UCI with weak athletic skills. In spite of this he was determined to be successful, and his father told me that whatever I wanted John to do, he would back me up. "The next five years, he's

. . . .

Don't pluck the apple while it is green; when
it is ripe it will fall of itself.
~ *Russian proverb*

. . . .

The delay of our dreams does not mean that
they have been denied.
~ *Sarah Ban Breathnach*

. . . .

Before I was ever in my teens, I knew exactly
what I wanted to be when I grew up. My goal
was to be the greatest athlete that ever lived.
~ *Babe Didrikson Zaharias*

. . . .

yours," his father said. John didn't waste time. He set his sights on his goal and went in a straight line towards it. Although he knew it would take a while, during his first three years he never complained or considered quitting, even when I didn't have him playing in games. He would sit next to me on the bench and listen intently as I coached the rest of the team. He would lift more weights and spend more time by himself working with a ball in the water than any other player. He took it as a great challenge to beat me to workout in the morning, and I'd find him waiting for me to open the door with a gleeful smile on his face. His willingness to be patient and persistent, and his sheer mental toughness, helped him become a leader on the team.

By his third year of college, he was playing in games, and I could see his talent emerging. He continued to work harder and longer than anyone else, and in 1989 he was a starter on the team that won the NCAA Championship. He scored a key goal against Stanford to get us into the championship round. Knowing how far he'd come, I was proud to see him make All American his senior year, and he has gone on in life with the same attitude he had in the water polo program, showing both patience and persistence. *EHN*

. . . .

In every triumph there's a lot of try.
~ *Frank Tyger*

. . . .

*It is our attitude at the beginning of a difficult
undertaking which, more than anything else,
determines it's successful outcome.*
~ *William James*

. . . .

*In the arena of human life, the honors and
rewards fall to those who show their good
qualities in action.*
~ *Aristotle*

. . . .

Success is the Best Revenge

Discontent and disorder are signs of energy and hope, not despair.
~Dame Cicely Veronica Wedgewood

When the boycott in 1980 prevented American athletes from competing in the Olympic Games, my wife Julie took it harder than I did. At the 1976 Olympics she had missed a medal in kayaking by only 1.3 seconds, the length of a boat, and had planned to try again at the 1980 Games. Being thwarted in her goal by politics was so deeply disappointing that it killed her enthusiasm for competition completely. She still paddled outrigger canoes for fun, but was no longer interested in serious racing.

In 1982 I entered the first Hawaiian Ironman triathlon, and at the last minute Julie decided to accompany me to Hawaii, to support me and to work on her tan. She had no idea that the course of her athletic career was about to change.

Julie has always run to stay in shape, but sometimes varies her routine by biking. The friend we were staying with in Hawaii was considered a favorite to win the women's race, and one day she asked if any of us would go on a training ride with her. When Julie said she'd be happy to go, the response was, "That's OK, I don't want to go that slow". As soon as I heard these words I knew it was the wrong thing to say to Julie. She was hurt and angry, and, although she said nothing, I saw a spark of defiance in her eyes. "You're going to do the Ironman, aren't you?" I asked her later. She nodded.

Fueled by indignation and anger, Julie began to train in earnest for the next Ironman, scheduled for October of the same year. (1982 was the only year in which Hawaii hosted two Ironman competitions; after the first race in February the organizers decided to move the event to accommodate competitors from around the world, and the

. . . .

We all boil at different degrees.
~ Ralph Waldo Emerson

. . . .

*Part of being a champ is acting like a champ.
You have to learn how to win, and not run
away when you lose. Everyone has bad
stretches, and real successes. Either way, you
have to be careful not to lose your confidence.*
~ Nancy Kerrigan

. . . .

*Guts are a combination of confidence,
courage, conviction, strength of character,
stick-to-itiveness, pugnaciousness, backbone,
and intestinal fortitude. They are mandatory
for anyone who wants to get to and
stay at the top.*
~ D. A. Benton

. . . .

race has taken place in October ever since.)

Julie had eight months to prepare, and nothing could hold her back, not even an accident five months before the race, in which she broke the tibia in her left leg when she was knocked off her bike by a car that ran a red light. What began as a desire to prove her athletic ability when provoked by a derogatory comment, soon became an outpouring of the anger she had suppressed since the Olympic boycott. All the pent-up frustration of the last few years was released in her training. She finally had her focus back, and in a way, the Ironman became a substitute for the goal that had been snatched away from her by the boycott in 1980.

Anger is a powerful emotion, and I saw first hand that when we direct it into the right channels, it can galvanize us into doing something positive. When Julie stood on the beach that balmy morning in October for the start of the race, she was surprisingly relaxed and confident. Her goal was to do the race and finish as best she could, purely as a personal challenge.

She began the race with a strong swim, and followed it with such a fast bike ride that she set a course record. Never again could anybody accuse her of being too slow on a bike. She went on to take the lead of the women's race within the first three miles of the marathon, and although she struggled in the latter stages of the run, she ended up winning the race in record time.

Redemption is sweet. *BL*

Chapter Six

Persistence

. . . .

All the fun is locking horns with impossibilities.
~ *Claes Oldenburg*

. . . .

Never give in, never give in, never, never, never, never—in nothing, great or small, large or petty—never give in except to convictions of honor and good sense.
~ *Winston Churchill*

. . . .

Everyone has his superstitions. One of mine has always been when I started to go anywhere, or to do anything, never to turn back or to stop until the thing intended was accomplished.
~ *Ulysses S. Grant*

. . . .

When You're Stuck Between a Rock and a Hard Place...Get Creative!

One of the secrets of life is to make stepping-stones out of stumbling blocks.
~ Jack Penn

Learning to deal with seemingly insurmountable odds is the key to success in just about everything. Whether it's sport, marriage, school, or a job, there are going to be problems, but if you're creative you can usually find a solution.

I've been coaching now for 46 years, and each year I try to do a better job of it. When I no longer feel I'm improving, then it will be time to quit. Six years ago it seemed as though the choice would not be mine.

I was used to walking up and down the pool deck, sometimes as far as three miles a night, yelling instructions to my players. This put tremendous pressure on my joints, and one day my doctor told me that I was bone to bone in my right knee and that a new joint would have to be put in. To have surgery and recover could take up to a year. I'd have to give up coaching for that year, or find a solution.

Pat Glasgow, a former player of mine, and now an Orange County Sheriff, told me a story about how prisoners awaiting trial find creative ways to lift weights. They take a mop, fill two buckets with water, put one on each end of the mop handle, and do bench presses. Where there's a will, there's a way.

I decided that I, too, could be creative. Instead of having surgery, I would buy a wheel chair, and by doing all my coaching sitting down, I would save my knees from the pounding they were taking every day on the cement of the pool deck The decision was a hard one, for I have

. . . .

Stand up to your obstacles and do something about them. You will find that they haven't half the strength you think they have.
~ *Norman Vincent Peale*

Never bend your head. Hold it high. Look the world straight in the eye.
~ *Helen Keller*

Happiness is not an absence of problems, but the ability to deal with them.
~ *Abe Lincoln*

. . . .

always prided myself on being independent and never asking for help, and I knew that once I was in a wheelchair, people who didn't know me would consider me an invalid. My knees, however, were more important than my ego, so I swallowed my pride. I also started doing weight work with my legs, to keep the muscles, tendons and ligaments as strong as possible.

The results have been good. My knees are tighter and stronger than they were six years ago, I now have less pain and what's more important, I'm still coaching. The hardest part about using the wheel chair is the humiliation I feel when people offer to help me. I know they have good intentions, but my ego gets a little bent out of shape when some pretty young lady wants to help me up a hill or open a door for me.

The other day an amusing situation occurred because of my wheelchair. I got to afternoon practice early so I stayed in the parking lot to clean up my '56 Ford pickup truck, (a great toy for an old man!). I then got into my wheelchair to head into practice. On the way in, some guy was lying down on the grass talking with a young lady. As I went by in my wheel chair he asked me, in a rather surly voice, if I could walk. To take verbal abuse is something I've never dealt with easily, so I told him that if I wanted to, I could get out of my chair and kick his ass, and would he like to find out? A couple of my players were walking in behind me, and it became the big laugh of the day for the team.

For me, persistence means that when you're caught between a rock and a hard place, you get creative and find a solution. You never give up. *EHN*

109

. . . .

Adversity has the same effect on a man that severe training has on the pugilist - it reduces him to his fighting weight.
~ Josh Billings

. . . .

When you can't change your fate, change your attitude.
~ Amy Tan

. . . .

Set your goals high and don't stop until you get there.
~ Bo Jackson

. . . .

When Things Go Wrong

Failure is success if we learn from it.
~ Malcolm Forbes

Sometimes things don't turn out as we'd like them to. That's just life. But in everything we do we have a choice: we can let an unpleasant experience bench us, or we can use it as motivation.

My first attempt at going to the Olympics in 1972 was an embarrassing failure. My kayak partner Tony Ralphs and I had won the National Championships in the 2-man kayak 500 and 1000-meter races the summer before, and during the course of the next year we trained hard and improved our times significantly. Everyone expected us to do well at the Olympic Trials in Illinois. In fact, we were favorites to make the Olympic team, and with high hopes I packed my bags and set off for the airport. It wasn't long before I realized that everything was going wrong.

Shortly after taking off for Chicago, our plane had to turn back to L.A. because of hydraulic problems. Hours late, we finally arrived in Chicago and I walked out of the air-conditioned terminal into a wall of oppressive heat. It was not only hot, but humid to the point that, within seconds, my clothes were soaked with sweat. I could hardly wait to have a shower, get comfortable, and settle down for the night.

We were to camp on a lake near Rockford, and we arrived to find that our tent had been set up in a grassy depression only a few feet away from the lake. Over the past few days it had rained quite heavily and the run-off had settled underneath our tent floor, creating a damp haven for mosquitoes. Swarms of them hovered above the lake, ready to move in for a feast. So much for getting comfortable!

Back in 1972 America's love affair with endurance sports hadn't

. . . .

*Concentrate on finding your goal, then
concentrate on reaching it.*
~ *Michael Friedsan*

. . . .

*You must have long term goals to keep you
from being frustrated by short-term failures.*
~ *Charles C. Noble*

. . . .

In the middle of difficulty lies opportunity.
~ *Albert Einstein*

. . . .

really made its appearance, and knowledge of sports medicine was meager. One of the guys in our group, thinking it would counter the effects of the heat and humidity, passed around salt tablets. Naive as we were, and always looking for an edge, it seemed like a good idea, so much so that if one tablet was good, two or three at a time would be even better. Big mistake! As we would find out later, the salt tablets acted as a diuretic, and instead of improving water retention and steeling us against the heat, we were actually dehydrating ourselves.

The whole week was a disaster. By the time the races began I felt physically drained, and my performance deteriorated with each race. The final blow came when I was not selected for the Olympic team. I was terribly disappointed. The fact that Tony did make the Olympic team, albeit by the skin of his teeth, compounded my failure, and although I was invited to stay for the training camp, I knew eventually I would have to go back home and face the people who had supported me and wished me luck before I left. Alone in my room that evening, I felt like crawling into a hole. Sometimes even Olympic hopefuls crash and burn.

Many times in my life things have not turned out as I expected, but I've learned to salvage what I can from the situation, patch my weaknesses with experience, and move on. I was tempted to shove the memories of that disastrous week in Illinois to the back of my mind, but I realized that if I chose to learn a lesson from every race that had turned sour on me, I could benefit from the experience. In four years I would have another chance to make the Olympic team. I would not give up.

That night, before a dinner to announce the U.S. Team, I took a T-shirt that read "1972 Olympic Team" in big block letters across the front and crossed out the year, printing 1976 boldly in its place. Montreal had replaced Munich as my destination, and for the next four years this T-shirt would remind me of my goal. *BL*

. . . .

If you view all the things that happen to you, both good and bad, as opportunities, then you operate out of a higher level of consciousness.
~ Les Brown

. . . .

The mind is its own place, and in itself can make a heaven of Hell, a hell of Heaven.
~ John Milton

. . . .

We cannot change our past. We cannot change the fact that people act in a certain way. We cannot change the inevitable. The only thing we can do is play on the one string we have, and that is our attitude.
~ Charles Swindoll

. . . .

Down, But Not Out!

'Tis easy enough to be pleasant, When life flows along like a song; But the man worthwhile is the one who will smile when everything goes dead wrong.
~ Ella Wheeler Wilcox

Ups and downs are a fact of life, but how we cope with them will reveal our character. It's ironic that we often learn more from our low points than we do from our highs; and if we can pull through when the chips are down, we will draw on that strength for the rest of our lives.

The big test for me came while I was training for the 1980 Olympics. Julie and I were determined to compete again, having had such a remarkable experience in the 1976 Olympic Games in Montreal, so as soon as we came back, we threw ourselves into training with a passion. Knowing that we had to make our goal "real" by talking about it, thinking about it, and making it a visible part of our lives, we hung Olympic posters around the house and even in the garage. We ordered a license plate for our new car that read "USSR 80", so that every day, whether coming or going, we would be reminded of our goal. People would see the license plate, pull up next to us, and give us the thumbs-up or a wave of encouragement, which spurred us to train even harder. I found a new partner, Chuck Lyda, and with Julie training alongside us for her own race, we worked steadily toward our goals. It was one of the high times of our athletic careers.

It is easy to maintain a positive attitude when everything is going well, but it is much harder when faced with an unpleasant situation that we can't control. At the end of 1979 the thunder of Russian troops in Afghanistan reverberated all the way to our doorstep as President Carter called for a boycott of the Olympic Games to protest the invasion. Congress backed him, the U.S. Olympic Committee was forced

. . . .

I feel as if I were a piece in a game of chess,
when my opponent says of it: That piece
cannot be moved.
~ *Soren Kierkegaard*

. . . .

Distance has the same effect on the
mind as on the eye.
~ *Samuel Johnson*

. . . .

You play the hand you're dealt.
I think the game's worthwhile.
~ *Christopher Reeve*

. . . .

to go along with it, and in a flash this political lightning bolt destroyed not only our dreams, but also the Olympic dreams of most of the top athletes in America. Although we knew the action was an attempt to forestall further aggression, we could hardly believe what was happening.

Attitudes towards us changed immediately, and the license plate we'd bought to motivate us became our albatross, a constant reminder of our disappointment. Now when people saw it, they stuck up their middle finger in an obscene gesture as we passed.

The U.S. Olympic Committee told the athletes that the Olympic trials to select a team would still take place. Some consolation. Chuck, Julie, and I, continued training, but the spark that had been there for so many years and kept us focused and motivated had gone out; we were only going through the motions. There was always a chance that at the last minute the team would be allowed to go, but deep down in our hearts we knew it was futile.

Looking back, I probably didn't handle the situation as well as I should have. It became hard to get out of bed in the morning to make it to workout, and to protest the boycott I decided to grow a beard. When I look back at photos of that time I hardly recognize the Neanderthal with the dull eyes as me. Apart from other athletes who were also dreaming of the Moscow Olympics, no one could fully comprehend our feelings. At the Olympic Trials in Vermont, neither Julie nor I qualified for the team, but it didn't really matter, for there were no Games to go to anyway. It was, without question, the lowest point of our athletic careers.

It would have been natural to quit the world of athletics altogether, as many Olympic hopefuls did. But somehow we knew we had to restore our attitudes. Knowing that one of the best ways to get out of a depression is to set another goal, we drove in silence back to California, each of us wondering what we could do next. At 34 I was too old to consider another Olympic Games, and yet sport was in my blood; I did not want to give it up. Julie was even more dispirited than I, for her chance to win a medal had been snatched away while she was in her prime.

Determined to climb out of my depression, I played the words "What can I do now?" over and over in my mind as we drove across the country. At a stopover in Minnesota, during an early morning run, the answer came to me: Triathlon. Swimming, biking and running. It

. . . .

History has demonstrated that the most
notable winners usually encountered
heartbreaking obstacles and yet triumphed.
They won because they refused to become
discouraged by their defeats.
~ *B.C. Forbes*

. . . .

Courage is the capacity to conduct oneself
with restraint in times of prosperity
and with courage and tenacity when
things do not go well.
~ *James V. Forrestal*

. . . .

Any time you try to win everything, you must
be willing to lose everything.
~ *Larry Czonka*

. . . .

was a new sport, but it played right into my past experiences as an athlete. Lifeguarding had given me experience in the ocean, biking I had enjoyed as a teenager, and as a runner I was fairly decent. In addition, I was used to the demands of long, exhausting workouts. Maybe this is where my future lay. I decided to enter a triathlon as soon as I got back, and somehow the journey home didn't seem so long any more.

People cope with setbacks in different ways. Initially Julie rejected athletics and threw herself into finishing her degree at Long Beach State. Although her goal was now academic rather than athletic, she too had a sense of purpose again. She began to accompany me whenever I went to triathlons, and at one of these, the Hawaiian Ironman, an idle comment sparked the revival of her athletic career. But that's another story. The important thing is that we learned how to climb out of our depression, and the experience made us stronger. *BL*

· ·

The difference between perseverance and obstinacy is that one often comes from a strong will, and the other from a strong won't.
~ *Henry Ward Beecher*

· · · · · · · · · · · · · ·

Nothing in the world can take the place of persistence. Talent will not; nothing is more common than unsuccessful men with talent. Genius will not; unrewarded genius is almost a proverb. Education will not; the world is full of educated derelicts. Persistence and determination alone are omnipotent.
~ *Calvin Coolidge*

· · · · · · · · · · · · · ·

Perseverance is not a long race; it is many short races one after another.
~ *Walter Elliot*

· ·

To the Limit, and Beyond

You become a champion by fighting one more round.
When things are tough, you fight one more round.
~ James J. Corbett

Only a handful of athletes can realistically have the goal of winning the Hawaiian Ironman. At one point I thought I could be a contender, but that was before I'd done the race. The course is one of the most difficult in the world, and regardless of your ability, it will chew you up and spit you out if you don't have the experience, or the guts, to conquer it. Top athletes have both. They experiment eagerly with different strategies that may give them an edge in the race, and they are brave enough to push their bodies to the limit to see if it will take their performance to a new level. Sometimes they bomb, big-time, but that's what we call experience.

In the 1984 Ironman I saw first hand the shaping of a great athlete as Mark Allen challenged the three-time champion Dave Scott in a dramatic one-on-one battle within the event. Even before the race, everyone knew it would be a duel between the two. Dave's strength was in the run, and he also had experience behind him, having won the race three times. Mark knew that to have a chance at winning he would have to build up a strong lead, and that was to be his strategy. I had decided not to compete that year, but saw the race close up from a car and a mountain bike that I'd borrowed for the day.

As I expected, the elite swimmers came out of the water in a pack, with Mark and Dave near the front. Mark jumped on his bike first, and set out doggedly on the 112-mile bike ride. From Kailua-Kona, the start of the race, it is 52 miles to the turn-around point at Hawi. I drove out there to watch them come by, stopping at various points along the

· ·

*We can do anything we want to do if we
stick to it long enough.*
~ *Helen Keller*

· · · · · · · · · · · · · ·

*Some men give up their designs when they
have almost reached the goal; while others,
on the contrary, obtain a victory by exerting,
at the last moment, more vigorous
efforts than ever before.*
~ *Herodotus*

· · · · · · · · · · · · · ·

*If you set a goal for yourself and are able to
achieve it, you have won your race. Your goal
could be to come in first, to improve your
performance, or just to finish the race
– it's up to you.*
~ *Dave Scott*

· ·

way, and as Mark rode into view I saw that according to plan he had built up a substantial lead over the rest of the competitors. Two more hours of exhausting heat and wind, and he came down the hill into town with an eleven minute lead over Dave. It seems that people always look better when they are leading a race, and Mark was looking great. He had never had an Ironman victory before, and it looked as though today might be his day.

The next time I saw them they were seven miles into the marathon, and Mark still looked good, powering up the hill leading to the lava fields with a strong stride that showed no sign of weakening. When Dave came by he had only made up a minute, and he looked at me with a slight shrug that seemed to say: "What can I do except keep going and see what happens?" With less than 20 miles to go I had the distinct feeling he wasn't expecting to catch up to Mark that day.

The most exciting thing about a race is that you never know what will happen. A couple of miles down the road, about a third of the way through the marathon, Mark began to falter and slow down. His stride shortened and he began to stagger like a helpless drunk, even coming to several stops. He seemed dazed and in shock, his skin was a ghostly gray and his eyes had glazed over. He was obviously in trouble.

Under extreme stress the body sometimes rebels and begins to shut down, and this was beginning to happen to Mark. In endurance sports this condition is called "The Bonk" or "hitting the wall". I was shocked to see how quickly the situation had changed. Dave caught Mark and passed him, but Mark was so focused on keeping his body in the race he didn't even seem to notice. At each aid station used every last muscle to lift a bucket of icy water and drench his failing body, hoping to revive it enough to trudge on. I hovered nearby, knowing he would be disqualified if I assisted him, but fearing he would lose his balance and end up in a heap with no one to help him.

The head course official that day was Dennis Haserat, an acquaintance of mine, and he pulled up and gave me official permission to stay with Mark. I was pleased to do so. I had been in awe of Mark's abilities for years and we had become pretty good friends, so as painful as it was to see him like this, it was a privilege to be able to follow him. I knew what he must be going through, for I too had walked long segments of the King Kam highway during the Ironman.

To this day I'm not sure Mark even knew I was there for the last ten to twelve miles of the race, but my admiration for him grew as I

. . . .

To be successful, you must decide exactly what you want to accomplish, then resolve to pay the price to get it.
~ *Bunker Hill*

. . . .

Preparing mentally takes more out of you than the physical aspects of it.
~ *Summer Sanders*

. . . .

There is nothing better than adversity. Every defeat, every heartbreak, every loss contains it's own seed, it's own lesson on how to improve your performance the next time.
~ *Og Mandino*

. . . .

saw his physical struggle and sensed his indomitable spirit. Bouts of diarrhea reduced him to squatting at the side of the road, but he would pull up his shorts and shuffle on valiantly. No longer was the race against Dave, it was now a battle between him and the course. Mark may have been broken physically, but he would not quit. If he was contemplating dropping out, he wasn't thinking coherently enough to make that decision, and step by step he moved toward the finish line. It was agonizing to watch. Perhaps he knew that the problem with quitting is that the challenge will not go away; sometime in the future it will be back again in one form or another. Far better to stay in the race, hold on to the dignity of finishing, and become wiser and stronger in the process.

Dave achieved another stunning Ironman victory and I was pleased for him, but what I remember most, and what inspires me when I'm struggling in my own races, is Mark's determination to finish. The best athletes are not just good when they're winning; they show their true character when they're down. Mark eventually came in 5th place, and although he was undoubtedly disappointed to have "bombed", he was able to learn from the experience. He went on to win the Hawaiian Ironman six times, and he and Dave Scott still have the reputation as the most accomplished male athletes in the sport of triathlon. *BL*

Chapter Seven

Responsibility

. . . .

To realize the value of ONE YEAR, ask a
student who failed a grade.
To realize the value of ONE MONTH, ask a
mother who gave birth to a premature baby.
To realize the value of ONE WEEK, ask the
editor of a weekly newspaper.
To realize the value of ONE HOUR, ask the
lovers who are waiting to meet.
To realize the value of ONE MINUTE, ask a
person who missed the train.
To realize the value of ONE-SECOND, ask a
person who just avoided an accident.
To realize the value of ONE MILLISECOND,
ask the person who won a silver medal in the
Olympics

. . . .

There is nothing of which we are apt to be so
lavish as of time, and about which we ought to
be more solicitous, since without it we can do
nothing in this world.
~ *William Penn*

. . . .

Learning the Value of Time

*Dost thou love life? Then do not squander time, for that
is the stuff life is made of.*
~ Benjamin Franklin

One thing I try to teach my players is the importance of learning time management, both in and out of the pool. The key to good performance in a water polo game is to be aware of the shot clock and the game clock at all times; if my athletes can understand that efficient use of time is critical in a sport, then it is an easy step for them to see the importance of time in everything they need to do. Hopefully, they'll learn not to waste it, but sometimes it's a hard lesson.

Recently I had a kid who was late for practice, and when he finally showed up, I had already locked the door to the weight room. He had wasted not only his valuable workout time, but my time as well, and I was annoyed. It was only February and the season was still six months away, but it's my belief that if you don't take the time in the off season to catch up and move ahead of the competition, you'll never do it once the season's begun. When he complained that he wanted to work out, I told him that since he hadn't respected either his time or mine, I was going to take away his privilege of working out for that day. Good players are good because they work hard and are responsible about time, and he needed to learn that, or find another water polo program. He grumbled a bit, but he's never been late again.

Every one of us has 1,440 minutes to spend each day, and it is our choice either to use them wisely or to fritter them away. I remember being impressed by stories about Woody Hayes, the famous Ohio State football coach, and how he read histories of wars and battles and related them to his coaching. I realized that to be an effective coach I had

. . . .

Guard well your spare moments. They are like uncut diamonds. Discard them and their value will never be known. Improve them and they will become the brightest gems in a useful life.
~ *Ralph Waldo Emerson*

. . . .

Life is not long, and too much of it must not pass in idle deliberation on how it shall be spent.
~ *Samuel Johnson*

. . . .

Character is the result of two things: mental attitude, and the way we spend our time.
~ *Elbert Hubbard*

. . . .

to read, too, but I was busy teaching, coaching and exercising and I thought I didn't have the time. Still, I knew I had to exercise my mind as well as my body, so I decided to be creative and find a way to carve out the time.

It occurred to me that we all have a lot of "dead" time in our lives. The first thing I got rid of was TV, and I started listening to books on tape instead. It is probably the single most important thing I've ever done for my mental and emotional growth. Over the past 13 years I've listened to over 600 books while working around the house, exercising on my stationary bike, or driving between my home and workout. Not only is it a great way to relax, but I can also absorb ideas from some of the best minds in literature. An outstanding combination, to my way of thinking. The average executive reads 0.8 books a year; I average 3 a month, and all in "dead" time. Not only have I become a better listener, which is very important if you want to learn from others, but now I can also use lessons from history to make some point to my players.

I believe that when you stop learning it is like quitting exercise: you are on a downward spiral to death. Dramatic maybe, but that is how strongly I feel about it. I like the fact that by not wasting time, I know I am improving my life, every minute of the day. *EHN*

. . . .

Every leader needs to have experienced and grown through following - learning to be dedicated, observant, capable of working with and learning from others, never servile, always truthful. Having located these qualities in himself, he can encourage them in others.
~ Warren G. Bennis

. . . .

Give the world the best you have, and the best will come back to you.
~ Madeline Bridges

. . . .

It is never too late to be what you might have been.
~ George Eliot

. . . .

Before We Can Lead, We Must Follow

No man is wise enough by himself.
~ Plautus

I've been calling myself "the Old Man" since I turned fifty, and I feel a huge responsibility for the growth and development of the athletes I think of as my "sons". We all need role models to help us grow into mature, productive adults, and young people are impressionable; they will watch and imitate whoever is around them. As a coach, I can have a far greater impact on young players than teachers or even some parents, mainly because of the time I spend in practice and the personal nature of the relationship I develop with my athletes. Spending twenty hours a week together, sometimes for four or five years, we get to know each other pretty well. I know that my players are watching me, whether I want them to or not, so I'd better be setting a good example.

I make it a point of honor always to be at workout on time. My players have my word I'll be there, and they know they can trust me. I usually leave at least an hour and a half before I have to be at the weight-room, because, as I tell my players, if my car breaks down or some beautiful lady wants to play games, I will still be at workout on time. The last comment always makes them laugh, but it emphasizes my point. If I failed to set an example, I would quickly lose my self-respect, and then my ability to lead and motivate others would cease to exist.

I know how important it is for my players to have someone to look up to and learn from, because I didn't have that as a child. When I was two years old my father's car was hit by a train, and he died several months later from the head injury he sustained. Although my mother

. . . .

If I can line up the people who, back through the ages, have gone at life in ways I greatly admire, then I can feel their strength supporting me, all their standards and values pointing the way in which I am to go.
~ *Bonaro W. Overstreet*

. . . .

Here is the simple but powerful rule...always give people more than they expect to get.
~ *Nelson Boswell*

. . . .

Conduct is three-fourths of our life and its largest concern.
~ *Matthew Arnold*

. . . .

used to tell me about him, how he was a strong man dedicated to his work and his family, it wasn't the same as having him around. I tried to live up to the image I had of him, but I had to learn by stumbling my way along, and I want to prevent my players from having to do that.

I'm always pleased when my former players come back to work out with us, because they are great role models for my team. When Evans, Kruse, Ibbetson, George, or Figueroa walk into the weight room, the atmosphere of the workout changes completely. They are living legends, part of "the family", and they help the younger players understand the sport they play and the value of what they are doing. They sell the program because it continues to work for them. The younger players listen to them and ask questions; they know the older athletes understand what they are going through and what they will have to face in the future.

Another type of role model I like my players to be around is a person who is older, successful in life, and who still values being fit. One of the best role models for my players is Eric Piper. His sons played water polo for Corona del Mar High School, so I used to see him at games. Years later he started to train in the masters swim program at UCI, and at the age of 66 he still works out every day and sets goals which athletes half his age would be happy to accomplish. When my players see Eric get out of the pool to go on a 6 mile run, they are impressed. I asked him once why he still makes fitness a part of his life. He said, "Some days I do wake up and wonder why I'm about to go out and punish my body with another run, but I never really answer the question, I just get into another workout. Fitness is me, and I like it. It is good for me, and I know it enables me to be more successful in every area of my life".

Eventually my players will become role models themselves, but before they can lead, they must follow. Ultimately, it's up to them whom they choose to emulate, but I hope that by surrounding my players with good role models they will become men of character, with the discipline, confidence, and self-respect to become successful in whatever they choose to do. It's a case of winning or losing in life, not just in sports. *EHN*

Although we heard the instructions: "You must work hard", "You must be more disciplined", and "You must be willing to pay the price",

. . . .

A mature man is his own judge. In the end,
his only form of support is being faithful to his
own convictions. The advice of others may be
welcomed as invaluable, but it does not free
him from responsibility.
~ Dag Hammarskjold

. . . .

We are shaped and fashioned by what we love.
~ Johann Wolfgang von Goethe

. . . .

A leader is one who knows the way, goes the
way, and shows the way.
~ John C. Maxwell

. . . .

what we really paid attention to was whether our coach was doing these things. Did he show up to practice? Was he prepared? Did he keep his promises? Was there energy and enthusiasm on the pool deck? Was he willing to make sacrifices for the good of the team? Did he ask us to do things he wasn't prepared to do himself? Self-discipline does not come naturally to anybody; it may be easier for some than for others, but it is always difficult. Looking back, I realize that what we saw and experienced influenced us more than what we heard.

~ *Gary Figueroa, U.C.I. Water Polo 1975-78*

. . . .

Be prepared, and you will be lucky.
~ Sun Tzu

. . . .

***We have forty million reasons for failure, but
not a single excuse.***
~ Rudyard Kipling

. . . .

***Always be nice to those you meet on your way
up, as you will meet them all on your way back
down.***
~ Peter Cutino

. . . .

For Want of a Tire, the Race was Lost

For want of a nail, the shoe was lost;
For want of the shoe, the horse was lost;
For want of the horse, the rider was lost;
For want of the rider, the battle was lost;
For want of the battle, the kingdom was lost;
And all for the want of a horseshoe nail.

~ English Nursery Rhyme

Have you ever noticed that sometimes it's the little things that ruin your day? The lesson in this old nursery rhyme is one I had to learn the hard way. I was at the Performing Arts Triathlon in Mission Viejo in 1987, and the race was going well, very well. I had a fast swim, and rode out of the transition area with Scott Tinley, one of the most notable triathletes in the sport and the favorite to win the race. We moved into the lead in the first mile of the bike ride, and I knew that if I stayed with Scott I had a good chance to be one of the top three finishers.

Suddenly I heard a sound dreaded by all cyclists: a pop and a hissing of air as a tire goes flat. I looked at Tinley's tire first, hoping that the flat was his problem to deal with, but as I slowed down, I knew it was mine. This was a disaster.

I had done seventy or eighty triathlons at that point and had never had a flat tire during a race. I usually carried at least one extra tire, though, just in case. During the Hawaiian Ironman in 1983, a disgruntled islander had thrown tacks on the bike course, causing a bunch of flats for many of the top athletes. I passed through safely, but other riders were not so fortunate. Marc Surprenant, one of the best triathletes from the East Coast, bumped to a halt with a flat tire and a dismayed look on his face. I dropped him one of my spares to help him get back into the

. . . .

***And oftentimes excusing of a fault doth make
the fault the worse by the excuse.***
~ William Shakespeare

. . . .

In fair weather prepare for foul.
Thomas Fuller

. . . .

If we are wise, let us prepare for the worst.
~ George Washington

. . . .

race, and afterwards, both he and his father thanked me for saving the day. I knew the importance of being prepared.

The morning of the Mission Viejo Triathlon, however, I had forgotten to bring a spare tire for my bike. By the time I realized my oversight, it was too late to do anything about it. I wasn't worried, though, because I was confident that if I needed a tire, someone would help me out like I'd helped Mark.

When my tire went flat I jumped off the bike and tried to get one of my fellow competitors, some of who were close friends, to drop a spare one for me. But the bikes whooshed on by, and no one would help. As they disappeared around the corner, I realized I was out of the race. Never before have I felt more disappointed or helpless during a competition. If I'd been carrying a spare, I would have lost three to five minutes changing the tire, but still I would have been in the top ten or fifteen finishers. At the very least I would have had a chance to finish the race. Now for want of a tire, my race was over.

Dejectedly, I made my way back to the transition area, where wave after wave of age-grouped athletes were still beginning their race. For the next forty minutes I watched them take off into the water, emerge onto the sandy beach, and race away on their bikes. When you are out there competing, time seems to fly by, but as I waited at the finish line for the leaders to come in, the race seemed like it would never end. Scott Tinley eventually added another easy victory to his list of accomplishments, and I learned a very important lesson: Be prepared. *BL*

. . . .

Safeguards are often irksome, but sometimes convenient, and if one needs them at all, one is apt to need them badly.
~ Henry Adams

. . . .

There are no shortcuts to any place worth going.
~ Beverly Sills

. . . .

The ability to accept responsibility is the measure of the man.
~ Roy L. Hunt

. . . .

The Day I Almost Lost My Head

Danger breeds best on too much confidence.
~ Pierre Corneille

John Howard, the three-time Olympic cyclist and 1981 Ironman winner, says, "There are only two types of bike riders: those who have crashed, and those who will". When I first started doing triathlons, twenty years ago, I was one of the "macho" riders who thought they could get by with a soft "hair-net" helmet. It was more important to feel comfortable and to look "cool" than to think about safety. These days I see things differently.

In 1988 I had the kind of crash that could have ended my life. I was racing in Big Bear, California, and for the first time was trying out a new style of Styrofoam helmet. Although light and colorful, it was designed with safety in mind. Up until that year I had been using an aerodynamic helmet shell that looked impressive but hadn't been approved by ANSI (American National Safety Institute).

The front wheel of my bike had only 18 spokes rather than the 36 on most wheels. It had performed flawlessly for me in races in France, South Carolina, Pennsylvania, and locally in California, and the only problem I'd ever had with it was just prior to the Big Bear race, when two spokes loosened. A bike shop mechanic tightened them for me, but unknowingly, he had over-tightened them.

Twelve miles into the fifteen-mile bike course around the lake, I took the lead in the race. As I was about to climb the last hill before crossing the levee at the east end of the lake, I heard a metallic popping sound. One of my spokes snapped, followed immediately by another. The spokes wrapped around the axle, the wheel collapsed, and within an instant the front forks sheered off. The knuckles on my left hand hit

. . . .

We are accountable only to ourselves for what happens to us in our lives.
~ *Mildred Newman*

. . . .

We have a Bill of Rights. What we need is a Bill of Responsibilities.
~ *Bill Maher*

. . . .

I will not surrender responsibility for my life or my actions.
~ *John Enoch Powell*

. . . .

the ground first, with such force that I flipped over and landed on the back of my head.

You hear of people's lives passing in front of them, but I distinctly remember only two thoughts going through my mind: "I'm going to hit my head", and "I hope this helmet works". At that point, I felt the Styrofoam helmet absorb the shock as if I were wearing a cushion; it was quite a remarkable feeling. I sat there for several minutes, holding my head and trying to stop the ringing, assessing the damage and watching as more and more athletes passed by with looks of horror on their faces at the sight of me on the ground. I was dazed and going into shock, but was able to get up and walk away. The helmet had shattered into three pieces, but my head was intact.

Later, I was diagnosed with a severely sprained neck, and although it took months to recover, it could have been much worse. The helmet I usually wore would have been totally ineffective in a crash like the one I'd just had. I'm shocked when I think that 96% of people who die in bike accidents are either not wearing a helmet, or have one that is not ANSI approved. I could have been one of them. These days I would no more consider riding my bike without my helmet than I would drive my car without buckling up my seatbelt. It definitely pays to "think safety", because it's definitely not "cool" to be paralyzed or dead. I was one of the lucky ones. *BL*

Chapter Eight

Confidence

· ·

It is an interesting question how far men
would retain their relative rank if they were
divested of their clothes.
~ *Henry David Thoreau*

· · · · · · · · · · · · · ·

Appearances aren't everything.
~ *American proverb*

· · · · · · · · · · · · · ·

A good archer is not known by his arrows,
but his aim.
~ *English proverb*

· ·

Beyond the "Rah-Rah"

In quietness and in confidence shall be your strength.
~ Isaiah 30:15

I have always been turned off by the "pep-rally" approach to sports, maybe because I grew up during World War II and saw photos of the elaborate Nazi rallies orchestrated by Adolf Hitler. Whatever the case, I have never felt we needed marching bands, cheerleaders and all the hoopla of the big time football schools. These things supposedly build the spirit of a team by giving them confidence and motivating them, but I have always believed that you should face the competition pumped up on the inside, full of the self-respect that comes from having had the discipline to work out day after day.

For over four decades, Levi's and T-shirts have been the attire for my water polo teams in whatever we have done, from coming to work-out to going to games. No ties or jackets on game day for us. If you've paid your dues in work and effort you don't need the fancy clothes and all the "rah-rah". In fact, focusing on these things may detract from your performance.

You should see the faces of the other team every time we walk onto the pool deck, dressed so casually. In a way it's like a game, a kind of "deceive the enemy", them thinking we are not "together" and us knowing that we have exactly what it takes. It makes the competition fun, and as long as I am coaching I see no reason why this should change. *EHN*

"Walking onto a pool deck with Newland, for me, was like being anointed. I felt invincible. Interestingly enough, whether I walked onto the pool decks at UCI, UCLA, Moscow, De Anza, Budapest, Stanford,

. . . .

We cannot achieve more in life than what we believe in our heart of hearts we deserve to have.
~ *James R. Ball*

. . . .

You've got to take initiative and play your game...confidence makes the difference.
~ *Chris Evert*

. . . .

Zeal is fit only for wise men, but is found mostly in fools.
~ *Thomas Fuller*

. . . .

or in a crummy spring tournament at Cypress College, it was like walking down the streets of Tombstone with Wyatt Earp. We were going to win and we were going to give the other team pain. Those were my proudest moments. In fact, I was very conscious of those "pool deck entries". Every one of them. Even the practices. This was our kingdom and we were with the king. We lived in his world. His world of early morning discipline. His world of pounding it daily in the weight room. His world of commitment. It was a very cool thing to stand next to Newland before a tournament championship game. I knew others were looking at us, just as I had watched the UCI guys when they had walked into Belmont Plaza Olympic pool the night UCI defeated UCLA for Newland's first NCAA championship. We had this aura about us for having survived Newland's daily hell, and now we were bringing this hell with us. It gave me a confidence that has never left me, and never will.

~ *Jim Kruse, U.C.I Water Polo 1972-73*

. . . .

*Sooner or later, those who win, are those
who think they can.*
~ *Richard Bach*

. . . .

*Show me a guy who is afraid to look bad, and
I'll show you a guy you can beat every day.*
~ *Lou Brock*

. . . .

*Experience tells you what to do; confidence
allows you to do it.*
~ *Stan Smith*

. . . .

Think Defeat and You'll Probably Get It

Confidence is a lot of this game, or any other.
If you don't think you can, you won't.
~ Jerry West

Sports psychology is part of every athletic program today, but when I began my career I had never heard of the phrase. Some of us had a positive attitude, and some of us didn't, but none of us realized what an important part our attitude played in our success. We know now that it is an essential ingredient in winning consistently. I found out that I still had a lot to learn in this area while playing in a water polo tournament at Golden West College, California, when I was about nineteen years old.

We were playing against Inland-Nu-Pike Long Beach, a team with several Olympians on its roster, and one of the best teams in the country. I was guarding Chuck Bittick, an Olympian in 1960 and a former world record holder in the backstroke. He was a Paul Bunyan in size, with a massive chest that made it very difficult to guard him. To me he was one of the "water polo gods", and although we were getting used to playing against top players like Chuck, he was still intimidating.

Early in the game, with us leading by a score of 2 to 1, I remember being in the water behind him, looking over his right shoulder at the ball and the other players, while at the same time trying to hold on to him as best I could. Hoping to pick up some pointers, I asked him casually how I was playing. He shrugged, as if to brush me off, so I added, "You might as well give me a tip, because you guys are going to beat us anyway". With that he turned and said in a fierce baritone voice: "Until you believe you can beat us, you never will!"

His comment froze the moment. I felt like a fool, but it was the

. . . .

*One who has lost confidence can
lose nothing more.*
~ *Boiste*

. . . .

*When you want to win a game, you have to
teach. When you lose a game, you have to
learn.*
~ *Tom Landry*

. . . .

*We are always teaching, and what we
consider least important, may be a student's
most significant lesson.*
~ *John Emme*

. . . .

most honest and true lesson he could have passed on. Sometimes it takes a slap in the face to jolt us out of a negative mindset, and that is how Chuck's comment hit me. It's a universal law of sports that if you think defeat, you very often get it, and he was experienced enough to know that. The game continued, and I don't remember the score, only that they did give us a beating.

I never spoke to Chuck again during a game, but I never forgot his comment. It was as though he'd opened a door for me, allowing my attitude to change. Several years later, my team finally matured enough to believe that we could beat them, and we did.

It's all too easy to slip into the habit of thinking in a negative way, questioning our ability and putting ourselves down. These days, when I am teaching, I try to convey the importance of thinking positive in all areas of life.

If you think you are beaten, you are.
If you think you dare not, you don't!
If you want to win, but think you can't,
It's almost a cinch you won't.

If you think you'll lose, you're lost;
For out in the world we find
Success begins with a fellow's will;
It's all in the state of the mind.

Life's battles don't always go
To the stronger and faster man,
But sooner or later the man who wins
Is the man who thinks he can.

~ Walter D. Wintle

Over the years Chuck and I have become good friends, and one day I mentioned the game at Golden West College. I told him how important his comment had been in molding my mental outlook, and ironically, what was literally a turning point in my athletic career, was not even a memory for him. *BL*

. . . .

Courage is the art of being the only one who knows you're scared to death.
~ *Earl Wilson*

. . . .

If you have no confidence in self, you are twice defeated in the race of life. With confidence, you have won even before you have started.
~ *Marcus Garvey*

. . . .

It's a lack of faith that makes people afraid of meeting challenges, and I believe in myself.
~ *Muhammad Ali*

. . . .

Set the Sail and Face the Wind

Do the thing you fear, and the death of fear is certain.
~ *Ralph Waldo Emerson*

When my son George was about nine or ten years old, he took sailing lessons during the summer. The final class was to be a sailing regatta, in which they would demonstrate everything they'd learned. On the day of the race a strong wind was blowing in from the desert (in Southern California these winds are called the Santa Anas, or "the devil's winds", because they are so hot and unpredictable). As time went by it started blowing really hard, about thirty miles an hour. George's mother dropped him off at the yacht club where he was to prepare the boat and sail down the harbor to the start-line, but back at the house she told me she was worried that the wind was too strong for him to sail in. I reassured her that the risk was pretty small that anything bad would happen to him; I had great confidence in his ability to deal effectively with the water.

A short while later the phone rang and it was George, saying it was too windy to sail, and asking his mother to pick him up. I went instead. As I drove up, I could tell by his face that he was scared.

"What's up?" I asked, and he replied that he wanted to go home. I never wanted to let my children off the hook when it came to doing something difficult, because I knew that facing challenges would develop their character and make them tough. So I told him he was supposed to be in a race, and he should get the boat rigged and get out there. I let him know that I thought he could handle it, and one by one I got rid of his excuses. If the boat tipped over, he could either get it back up again or swim to shore; if the mast broke I would buy him a new one. I helped him believe in himself, and in the end he made the

· ·

With confidence, you can reach truly amazing heights; without confidence, even the simplest accomplishments are beyond your grasp.
~ *Jim Loehr*

I think it's the mark of a great player to be confident in tough situations.
~ *John McEnroe*

If you truly feared failure, you'd be very successful.
~ *Barbara Sher*

· ·

decision to give it his best shot.

I watched him struggle through the choppy water to the starting line, and when he got there he found that the race had been cancelled. It was too windy, and no one else was there. But he was! He felt so good about himself, knowing that he hadn't given up. It was just a small incident, but not letting him quit was probably the best gift I ever gave him. It was the first step in learning to believe in himself, and he gained a lot of self-respect.

At some time in our lives most of us have to face a Santa Ana wind. We can choose to be intimidated and stay indoors, or we can face the challenge, stretch our abilities, and grow stronger from the experience. I'm glad my son chose the latter. *EHN*

I remember being really scared because it was blowing so hard, but after our discussion I rigged the boat and headed out. I began to focus on the positive side of the situation rather than the negative, and once I was out there I had a great time. The boat was cranking and I lost my fear, because all the things that had worried me had been pointed out to me in a way that gave me the confidence to overcome them. When I arrived, the regatta had been cancelled due to the high winds. The whole experience gave me a lot of confidence and taught me how to overcome the fear of competition in extreme conditions. It's something that I remember when I am competing, and when my children express fear in competition.

~ George Newland U.C.I Water Polo 1974-78

. . . .

When I was young I was amazed at Plutarch's statement that the elder Cato began at the age of eighty to learn Greek. I amazed no longer. Old age is ready to undertake tasks that youth shirked because they would take too long.
~ W. Somerset Maugham

. . . .

To resist the frigidity of old age, one must combine the body, the mind, and the heart. And to keep these in parallel vigor, one must exercise, study, and love.
~ Bonstettin

. . . .

If wrinkles must be written upon our brows, let them not be written upon the heart. The spirit should never grow old.
~ James A. Garfield

. . . .

Looking Forward at Fifty

Use age as an advantage, not as an excuse.
~ L. J. Hawthorne

Fifty is a milestone for most of us; a time when we start to question whether we can still set goals and achieve them, whether we still have what it takes. Being "over the hill" is a relative term, because everybody's hill is different, but for me, having been a competitive athlete for most of my life, I feared that when I turned fifty I would lose the ability to participate in events with the same intensity as before. Seven years previously I had entered the first International Triathlon Union (ITU) World Championships and had lost to a Frenchman, by a mere 23 seconds. In my mind he will always be "The Phantom", for I was never aware that he had passed me. Right up to the time I was on the podium to receive my medal, I thought I had won the race, and the bitter disappointment I felt at coming second had haunted me for years. Although I wanted to enter the race again, a giant question mark now shadowed my confidence. I was fifty; did I still have what it took to be successful athletically? One advantage of getting older is that with maturity comes perspective, and when I decided to race in the ITU World Championships in Cleveland, Ohio, in the fall of 1996, I knew it would be a defining point in my life. I was prepared to accept the challenge.

As we age, it is definitely harder to do what used to come easily, but I found that what I had lost in physical strength, I had gained in mental discipline. I trained hard, struggling to get back to a high level of fitness. It helped a lot to have training partners who were all younger than I was and could push me to the limit on every ride. Twice a week we would ride an all-out 23-mile workout that finished up Newport

. . . .

It is not how old you are, but how you are old.
~ *Marie Dressler*

. . . .

Youth is not a time of life, it is a state of mind.
People grow old only by deserting their ideals
and by outgrowing the consciousness of youth.
Years wrinkle the skin, but to give up
enthusiasm wrinkles the soul. You are as old
as your doubts, your fears, and your despair.
The way to keep young is to keep your faith
young, your self-confidence young, and your
hope young.
~ *Dr. J. F. Phelan*

. . . .

Age is a matter of feeling, not of years.
~ *George William Curtis*

. . . .

Coast Road, a tortuous 2½-mile hill that drains you of every ounce of energy. My goal was to finish ahead of at least one of the group. Because of these friends - Bob Cuyler, Steve "Scoots" Walters, John Brazelton, Bob Kinney, Mike Pugh, Sue Davis, Dave Fier, Dan Neyenhuis, and Bob Stipp - we routinely finished the ride in less than an hour; great mental and physical preparation for the World Championships.

On the day of the race, what I had planned for and trained for became a reality. After a 500-yard warm-up swim in a local hotel pool with a friend of mine, Fred Millard, I got off to a good start in the race. The water conditions in Lake Erie were perfect, and I knew I was swimming well when I "dropped" two guys along the way. Losing no time in the transition to the bike, I cranked through the residential streets of Cleveland, and as I started the first loop of the highway I had a fortuitous encounter. Bob Belzer, a former World Champion in his age group and a good friend of mine, was starting his second loop of the course. We rode together for about five miles, and by pushing the pace, he definitely helped my performance.

I had driven the running course earlier so I knew what to expect: mainly flat, but with a couple of major hills. Since running is not my strength, I was surprised and encouraged when I began to pass people. The run actually seemed shorter than the 6.2 miles, and as I approached the finish line I knew without doubt that this time I would win. How I enjoyed the last few yards! It was one of those glorious moments when expectation and accomplishment fuse, and the experience was cathartic. My victory banished the disappointment of losing to the "Phantom", but more importantly, it dispelled my doubts about aging. I had proved to myself that all was not lost, and that at fifty years of age I could still train hard and be competitive. In the grand scheme of world sport, winning an age group world championship is pretty insignificant, but to me, grappling with what it means to get older, it meant a lot. It felt like a giant yoke had been lifted from my shoulders.

Today I take on projects and set goals with renewed confidence. I've learned that we can lead active, successful lives at any age if we have the desire to do so and the willingness to work at it. Life at fifty can be just as exciting as when we were teenagers, the difference is that now we don't take it for granted. *BL*

Chapter Nine

Trust

. . . .

Trust, like the soul, never returns,
once it is gone.
~ *Publilius Syrus*

. . . .

Trust is the lubrication that makes it possible
for organizations to work.
~ *Warren Bennis*

. . . .

You may be deceived if you trust too much, but
you will live in torment if you
don't trust enough.
~ *Frank Crane*

. . . .

The One Thing You Must Never Lose

Fire, Water, and Trust were walking in the woods and talking about what they should do if they got separated. Fire said, "Look for smoke, that's where I'll be". Water said, "look for the green grass and flowers, and that's where I'll be". Trust said, "You'd better not lose me at all, because if you do, you may never get me back again."

In athletics, players come and go, and every year I start from the beginning to build a new team. The strongest teams I've coached have one thing in common: trust.

I firmly believe that without trust, a team will be a group of individuals, and nothing more, so I work hard to establish in my players the good habits that will allow their teammates to trust them. There are no secrets. Trust is not easy to establish, nor is it easy to maintain. Developing trust takes time, and it is built on what a player does every single day in practice. By having the self-discipline to show up to early morning practice, to work hard even when he doesn't feel like it, to use his time effectively, and to not dissipate his body with alcohol or drugs, a player lets his teammates know that they can rely on him. If he misses practice, comes late, goofs off while he's there, or lets his anger get out of control, the rest of the team will probably not say anything, but, in a very subtle way, their trust in that player is diminished. As a result, when the players find themselves in a tight game in which they need to trust each other to perform well, they will remember who has proved unreliable in the past, and they will not trust him in the game. Individual athletes will step up and try to do it all themselves, instead of working together and having confidence in the team as a whole. Without trust in each other, the performance of the team will never reach its potential.

As Woody Allen said, "Life is 90% just showing up." Trust is very

· ·

No, I don't understand my husband's theory of relativity, but I know my husband, and I know he can be trusted.
~ Elsa Einstein

· · · · · · · · · · · · · ·

If you can't trust people, who can you trust?
~ Hohn Widdiconbe

· · · · · · · · · · · · · ·

Woe to the man whose heart has not learned while young to hope, to love – and to put its trust in life.
~ Joseph Conrad

· ·

fragile, and although players can like their teammates, whether they trust them will depend on their actions in the past. No excuse for failing to be there at practice will bring back the trust. The bottom line is to do what you've said you'll do. This is a brutal reality, but it is as true as anything I know. *EHN*

Playing water polo I learned that trust is made up of many small actions, and that it has to be worked at constantly to be maintained. I learned that trust is earned, and that it takes time to develop. As a result, I respect people's trust in me, and I seek to maintain that trust much more seriously than many people my age. I learned that when you say you will do something, you always perform. If I say that I will be somewhere at a certain time, I make sure I am there and ready. When I question whether one person can always come through and be depended on, I think of Newland. I remember that in all my time with him, not once has he failed to complete something he said he would, and he always performed to the utmost of his abilities. As a team we learned to trust him, and wanting him to trust us too, we became better people.
~ Jean Michel, U.C.I. Water Polo 1993-96

During my college years of playing water polo, Ted Newland would try to convince us of the importance of trust in a game. After every game we won, and after every game we lost, he would drill into us that the key to success was being able to trust each other in the pool, that accountability was everything. Winning the NCAA Championship in 1989 helped me understand what he meant. Each of us did what we were supposed to do, not less, and not more; I know that being able to trust each other allowed UC Irvine to win the title.
~ Pablo Yrizar Barranco, U.C.I. Water Polo 1989-92

. . . .

Should you shield the valleys from the windstorms, you would never see the beauty of their canyons.
~ Elisabeth Kubler-Ross

. . . .

The price of greatness is responsibility.
~ Winston Churchill

. . . .

Responsibility is the thing people dread most of all. Yet it is the one thing in the world that develops us, that gives us fiber.
~ Frank Crane

. . . .

Letting Go, So They Can Grow

Trust men and they will be true to you; treat them greatly and they will show themselves great.
~ Ralph Waldo Emerson

Giving up control is not easy for anyone, whether a coach, a parent or a business owner. What it comes down to is trust. I feel very strongly that part of being a good coach is learning to give up the reins and let the athletes take responsibility for themselves. When I believe I've taught my players enough to launch out on their own I have to stand aside, point out the path ahead, and say: "Go!". Bottom line is, if they succeed, not only will we win games, but the players will probably be successful in life. It was my athletes who taught me this lesson.

In 1970 I was preparing my team to play in the NCAA Championship game against UCLA. It was the first time we had made the finals, and I knew it was important to call team meetings to work out issues such as why we weren't getting good shots and how we could improve. Although my players would throw in their comments, I was responsible for running the meeting and would always have the final say.

Being a coach is very much like being a parent: you know you have to let go sometime, but the key is to judge when the time is right. There is a big difference between coaching high school and college; the college athletes are no longer boys and at some point they need to start shouldering some of the responsibility for the team. So one day I suggested to my team captain, Ferdy Massimino, that they should hold a players-only meeting. This was a first, but I realized it's all too easy to be a control freak, especially when it's a big game, and I decided that if I'd done a good job as a coach the team would become stronger when they realized that I trusted them to meet on their own. When

. . . .

The man who trusts other men will make
fewer mistakes than he who distrusts them.
~ Camillo di Cavour

. . . .

The only way to make a man trustworthy is to
trust him.
~ Norman Thomas

. . . .

The trust that we put in ourselves makes us
feel trust in others.
~ La Rochefoucauld

. . . .

they're in the water competing they have to work as a team, so why not let that process begin sooner? I was confident they could do it.

My team didn't disappoint me. Something about conducting their own meeting helped pull them together, and although it was a close game, we beat UCLA 7-6 to win our first NCAA Championship.

I've come to think that when we hand out too many crutches to our kids, all it does is hold them back. We need to let them go, let them fall over, then celebrate with them when they get back up and can stand alone. I strongly believe that it's my job to make young people step up and take responsibility. Encouraging my teams to hold their own meetings when they reach a certain level is a step in that direction. *EHN*

Newland decided that a players-only meeting was a good idea. This surprised me a little, for I didn't expect him to willingly let go of some of his control. In retrospect I see that he recognized the value of a team finding a sense of purpose and solidarity on its own, something every team must accomplish at some point. It was a great learning experience for us all.
~ Mike Martin-Sherrill, U.C.I. Water Polo, 1967-71

Chapter Ten

Teamwork

. . . .

I love to hear a choir. I love the humanity, to see the faces of real people devoting themselves to a piece of music. I like the teamwork. It makes me feel optimistic about the human race when I see them co-operating like that.
~ Paul McCartney

. . . .

Friendship is the only cement that will ever hold the world together.
~ Woodrow Wilson

. . . .

Tolerance and celebration of individual differences is the fire that fuels lasting love.
~ Tom Hannah

. . . .

Outriggers in Paradise – Breaking Down Cultural Barriers

No man is an island, entire of itself; every man is a piece of the continent, a part of the main.
~ John Donne

Every four years the summer Olympics begins with a formal ceremony. Clusters of athletes in different colored uniforms march around the track carrying the flag of their country, and we are conscious that here is a collection of very different nations coming together in rivalry, a friendly rivalry, but fiercely competitive all the same. Tension is high as the torch is lit and the Games begin.

The closing ceremony, in contrast, is like one big international party. It doesn't seem to matter at this point if you've won a medal or not, you have a common bond in the Olympic experience. All the athletes have found friends from other countries and many now walk arm in arm. Some have traded sweat jackets or caps in a gesture of goodwill, and the atmosphere is informal and relaxed. In my experience, this is the beauty of sport: it brings people together and quickly helps them transcend barriers of race, age, and culture.

After the Olympic boycott in 1980 I still wanted to be involved in competitive sport, so I joined the Imua Outrigger Canoe Club in Newport Beach, California. When we were invited to participate in the inaugural Tahiti International Outrigger Race, I hoped it would be an event, like the Olympics, that would foster a spirit of goodwill.

The race was held in conjunction with the Bastille Day Festival on July 14th, which all French Territories celebrate, and although several teams from Hawaii were going, we would be the only team from the mainland. We had heard stories about the beauty of Tahiti, but none of

. . . .

Good humor is a tonic for mind and body. It is the best antidote for anxiety and depression. It is a business asset. It attracts and keeps friends. It lightens human burdens. It is the direct route to serenity and contentment.
~ *Grenville Kleiser*

. . . .

Men become friends by a community of pleasures.
~ *Samuel Johnson*

. . . .

Look at people; recognize them, accept them as they are, without wanting to change them.
~ *Helen Beginton*

. . . .

us had been there. Knowing that reality often fails to live up to fantasy, we were surprised when in every respect Tahiti was better than we had imagined. The weather was balmy and clear, the islands were lush with a covering of thick green forest, and the water was an iridescent turquoise blue. The air was thick with the sweet fragrance of plumeria flowers, and the people were as friendly and happy as any I had ever met, not to mention that most of the women were tanned, gorgeous, and wore brightly colored batik wrap-around pareos from the waist down, with nothing above. We thought we'd died and gone to heaven.

Besides cock fighting, outrigger canoe racing is a favorite national pastime in Tahiti. The Tahitians had organized a distance race, a 65-mile journey around the island of Moorea that would begin and end in the port of Papeete, the capital city of Tahiti. My team found out that to celebrate Bastille Day there would be a regatta in Papeete harbor a couple of days before the distance race, and although we had not prepared for it, in the spirit of the day we decided to give it a go.

Everything from one-man canoes to sixteen person Dragon Boats would be competing in the regatta, but the first race was in a one-man outrigger. Not knowing how to handle this kind of boat, some of us paddled around in circles, and others fell over and sank. We began to laugh at ourselves, and the Tahitians laughed too, wondering what kind of athletes we were. Their suspicions were confirmed in the last race of the day, the Dragon Boat race. Hundreds of paddlers were on the water, maybe 40 boats in all. Our team got off to a good start, but within a few hundred yards we were taking on water and our boat sank lower and lower until the bow submerged and we came to a halt. Sitting in water up to our necks, we laughed and cussed all at the same time. Now more than ever we had something to prove in the race around Moorea.

The boats we were used to paddling in California were modeled on the Hawaiian Malia boats that were originally designed for fishing: their round bottoms made for good handling in waves, but they were not built to go fast. The Tahitian boats, on the other hand, are built for one thing: speed. They are like stilettos in the water: one paddle stroke and the boat seems to glide forever. For us, paddling the Tahitian boat that we had borrowed for the race was like driving a Porsche versus an old pick-up truck filled with sand.

The key to success in outriggers is timing, conditioning, team-

. . . .

Only connect.
~ *E.M. Forster*

. . . .

The medals don't mean anything and the glory doesn't last. It's all about your happiness. The results are going to come, but my happiness is just loving the sport and having fun performing.
~ *Jackie Joyner Kersee*

. . . .

Coming together is a beginning, staying together is progress, and working together is success.
~ *Henry Ford*

. . . .

work, and choosing the right course. Luckily, these were our strengths. As we lined up just outside the harbor entrance to Papeete, we saw there were over 60 boats in the race, most from Tahiti and its surrounding islands, but some from further away, such as the island of Moaroa where the French used to test their nuclear bombs. To the surprise of everyone but us we got off to a great start, and when we approached the island of Moorea, about seven miles into the race, we were in third place.

The jagged, verdant peaks of Moorea sweep up from calm lagoons formed by the reefs that protect the island from the pounding surf. At certain points we were so close to these reefs that we would rise up with each swell and hang for a few seconds as the wave passed underneath us and crashed with a thunderous explosion onto the reef. A soothing mist from the wave would blow over us as we paddled on. Inspired by the spectacular surroundings, we moved into second place; by the time we rounded Moorea we had surged into the lead.

We never let up, and as we entered the harbor of Papeeti six hours after the start, we were the only boat to be seen. Thousands of islanders lined the docks and shoreline and although they must have been stunned to see that the Americans had defeated their crews, they cheered wildly in appreciation of our effort.

The party that followed was also a surprise. Wherever we went people gave us Hinano beers or Mai Tai cocktails made with what could only be described as fermented gasoline, and as music from the Tahitian bands reverberated across the water, we knew for a moment what it must have been like for Captain Cook and his crew to fall in love with a South Pacific paradise and its people. Everyone shook our hands and gave us bear hugs, and we laughed together, sharing the moment not as competitors, but as friends bound by the common experience of sport. *BL*

. . . .

I love the winning, I can take the losing, but
most of all I love to play.
~ *Boris Becker*

. . . .

I don't psyche myself up. I psyche myself
down. I think clearer when
I'm not psyched up.
~ *Steve Cauthen*

. . . .

If you make every game a life and death
proposition, you're going to have problems.
For one thing, you'll be dead a lot.
~ *Dean Smith*

. . . .

The Experience of a Team

The way a team plays as a whole determines its success. You may have the greatest bunch of individuals in the world, but if they don't play together, the club won't be worth a dime.
~ Babe Ruth

Someone once asked me which I liked best, individual or team sport. I didn't even have to think about it. Some of my best memories are of competing in the team sports of water polo and outrigger canoe racing. Although there is a certain glory in winning something as an individual, being part of a team is much more appealing to me. I like the camaraderie that comes from knowing that we are in it together, vulnerable as a group, and relying on each other to do our best. Over time you learn who is reliable and who can perform under pressure, and you learn to trust each other, one of the most critical factors in developing a strong team.

They say that soldiers who go to war share such intense experiences that they are linked together for life, and although sport is not a life or death situation, I know that similar feelings can unite the members of a team. A closeness develops that can last a lifetime; some of my best friends today are the guys I played water polo with over thirty years ago.

I hadn't played on a water polo team for years, but in 1998 one of my best friends, Bob Nealy, decided to get a group together to compete in the World Masters Games hosted by Nike in Portland, Oregon. Although I knew most of the guys on the team, we had had no time to train together and I wondered if we'd be able to pull it off. The favorite to win this tournament was a team from Croatia consisting of some former Olympians from the Yugoslavian gold medal team of the 80's,

. . . .

The person who figures out how to harness
the collective genius of his or her organization
is going to blow the competition away.
~ *Walter Wriston*

. . . .

We do not so much need the help of our
friends as the confidence of their help in need.
~ *Epicurus*

. . . .

We must, indeed, all hang together or, most
assuredly, we shall all hang separately.
~ *Benjamin Franklin*

. . . .

so we definitely had our work cut out for us.

We were to play six games over three days. Our first few games, though victories, were very sloppy, since we weren't familiar with each other's moves. We would rush shots, throw the ball away, and not cover on defense. But as the week wore on we began to learn each other's moves and to communicate better. As a player I seem to perform above my ability as part of a team, because when I know people are relying on me I push myself harder. I think that was true for the others, too. The trust was beginning to build.

The first time we played the Croatian team, they capitalized on our mistakes and lapses in defense and we lost 6-8, but the game was a close one and it gave us confidence that we were improving. The next morning we won a game that got us to the finals. That afternoon we would have a repeat match with the Croatians.

Before the game, we got together for a team discussion to determine our strategy. Steve Hammond, one of the best goalies in the world, said: "Let's go out and play like we can, and have fun!" At that, Mike Garibaldi, one of our field players, said: "Hell with having fun, let's win". I commented that it's hard to have fun and lose at the same time, and for the first time that week we seemed united as a team, really "together" and focused on winning. The joking seemed to loosen us up, and we played our best game, relaxed, but focused. We won the gold medal by a score of 9-7. What satisfaction! Nothing compares with the "high" of being able to celebrate a victory with your teammates, whether you've known them for years or for just a few weeks, and I hadn't had so much fun in decades. We laughed together, hugged each other, and had a few beers. We felt like we were twenty years old again. *BL*

. . . .

Alone we can do so little; together we can do so much.
~ *Helen Keller*

. . . .

The achievements of an organization are the results of the combined efforts of each individual.
~ *Vince Lombardi*

. . . .

The nice thing about teamwork is that you always have others on your side.
~ *Margaret Carty*

. . . .

Together Everyone Achieves More

A single arrow is easily broken, but not ten in a bundle.
~ Japanese proverb

In all my years of coaching college athletes, only two players have ever joined a fraternity. The rest didn't need to. My players have always gained a feeling of belonging and acceptance from the team. I'm always interested to see that even though I've never required my players to hang out together or be best friends, strong bonds develop between them that often last a lifetime. It's like war: win together, lose together, but be united.

It all begins in the weight room. My players spend hundreds of hours during the year working out and gaining the strength to overpower other teams, and in the process, they are building much more than just muscle mass. Every time they show up and work out hard, they are proving themselves to their teammates. Trust develops, and they know that when things get tough, they will be able to rely on each other and pull through.

Every player on my team knows he is an active contributor to the success of that team. To feel important, to feel useful, and to be involved are key to developing self-respect and self-worth, qualities all too rare in this day and age. An individual can enjoy his or her accomplishments, but as part of a team, the emotion is enhanced. It really is a case of "together everyone achieves more".

My players share in each other's lives, and they seem to take pride in helping and supporting each other through both the down times and the good times. Almost every year one of them has to deal with a serious problem, often the divorce of his parents, and I've found that they benefit greatly from sitting down and talking to one or two teammates

. . . .

If a team is to reach its potential, each player
must be willing to subordinate his personal
goals to the good of the team.
~ Bud Wilkinson

. . . .

A particular shot or way of moving the ball
can be a player's personal signature, but
efficiency of performance is what wins the
game for the team.
~ Pat Riley

. . . .

I think any player will tell you that individual
accomplishments help your ego, but if you
don't win, it makes for a very, very long
season. It counts more that the team
has played well.
~ David Robinson

. . . .

or former players who have been through the same difficult situation. By discussing the problem with someone he knows he can trust, the player gets a clearer picture of the situation. He learns that someone with the same problem has lived through it, and although talking doesn't necessarily solve anything, he knows he's not going through it alone.

It's most gratifying to me to see my players celebrating together. The other day I went to a wedding, and sixteen ex-players attended. The best man, Pablo Yrizar, came all the way from Mexico City. That's the kind of feeling my athletes have for each other; we are a large family from the oldest to the youngest. My younger players have great respect for the alumni, because they know that anyone who has hammered through my program must be a worthwhile human being who understands the value of self-discipline and self-motivation. The older players respect the younger players, too, and a bond of respect and trust is established that goes well beyond the boundaries of the pool.
EHN

The thing that was so great, so beautiful, so wonderful...is that we were part of a team. We had a chance to be more than the sum of all our parts and our efforts. When you have the opportunity to have this kind of fun and happiness, take advantage of it! Get excited when someone scores a goal or makes a play. When you are competing intensely but also having fun, you can swim and play hard defense for four quarters and have more energy when it's all over. Most people never experience the feeling of becoming more than they are as an individual by being part of a unique group, and maybe one person out of the entire team will find some working environment where they get that feeling again. There were guys I didn't like, guys that I was envious of, but that was all so petty. So small. The big thing was that we were a TEAM.
~ *Peter Muller, U.C.I. Water Polo 1991-95*

Chapter Eleven

Perspective

. . . .

It is not the critic who counts. Not the man who points out how the strong man stumbled, or where the doer of deeds could have done better. The credit belongs to the man who is actually in the arena, whose face is marred by dust and sweat and blood; who strives valiantly; who errs and come short again and again; who knows the great enthusiasms, the great devotions; who spends himself in a worthy cause. Who, at the best, knows in the end the triumph of high achievement, and who at worst, at least fails while daring greatly, so that his place shall never be with those timid souls who know neither victory nor defeat.

~ Theodore Roosevelt

. . . .

The ideal man bears the accidents of life with dignity and grace, making the best of circumstances.

~ Aristotle

. . . .

How to Win, Even When You Lose

In every difficult situation is potential value. Believe this, then begin looking for it.

~ Norman Vincent Peale

None of us likes to lose. In his book "A Passionate State of Mind" Eric Hoffer says, " There is no loneliness greater than the loneliness of a failure. The failure is a stranger in his own house". I know exactly what he's talking about.

I remember an event in 1985 in which we were geared up to play Stanford in the NCAA Championship finals. I felt confident that if we played our game and kept our focus, we would have it in the bag.

The match with Stanford that night was a fairly even one, but at the end, with the game tied and only nine seconds left, our guy, Jeff Campbell, scored. A beautiful backhand shot that stung the net when it landed.

The place went wild. My players, in the water and on the bench, went wild as well. The team smelled victory, and overwhelmed with emotion they slapped each other on the back and gave high fives all around. In the confusion there was no time to set the defense - in those days only the team with the ball could call a time out. The teams lined up in the middle of the pool and waited for the ball to be tossed to Stanford. With only nine seconds left, there wasn't time for Stanford to swim down the pool, set their offense and get a good shot off. Their only chance was to shoot from the half-court, and hope for a miracle.

For some reason our goalie, Mark Maizel, who had played brilliantly up to that point, came out of the cage. Certain they would shoot from outside, he was probably trying to cut down the angle. I never asked him, but whatever the reason it was a bad decision. Matt Tingler,

. . . .

In adversity, remember to keep an even mind.
~ *Horace*

. . . .

*It is by studying little things that we attain the
great knowledge of having as little misery and
as much happiness as possible.*
~ *Samuel Johnson*

. . . .

*What's gone and what's past help,
Should be past grief.*
~ *William Shakespeare*

. . . .

one of Stanford's best players, made a perfect lob-shot from outside and it went in. Once again we were tied. There was one second on the game clock.

The crowd went wild again, but this time it was Stanford jumping up and down, celebrating their last second reprieve. My team was utterly deflated. We tried to get our composure and focus back between the end of the regulation game and the overtime period, but it was too much to expect with emotions running out of control. We struggled in the overtime and fell apart on defense. We lost the championship.

I replayed the game over and over in my mind, more than any game I have ever coached. I was very frustrated, and very angry about losing.

Many years later, with the advantage of perspective, I know that losing has its benefits. When a team wins, they usually celebrate the victory and then put it aside; they may replay the winning shot over and over, but they tend to forget the game itself and don't necessarily learn from it. When they lose, they mull over all the little mistakes that added up to defeat, and discuss what could have been done to change the outcome. If you take the time, you can learn a lot. Our loss to Stanford improved our strategy and at the same time strengthened the team itself, and I felt closer to that team than any I had won with.

As "the Old Man", I still hate to lose, but now I know that it isn't fatal. The sun will rise the next day as it always has, and you just survive your emotions, set new goals, and move on. *EHN*

. . . .

If you want to take your mission in life to the next level, if you're stuck and you don't know how to rise, don't look outside yourself. Look inside. Don't let your fears keep you mired in the crowd. Abolish your fears and raise your commitment level to the point of no return, and I guarantee you that the Champion Within will burst forth to propel you toward victory.
~ Bruce Jenner

. . . .

Live out of your imagination, not your history.
~ Stephen Covey

. . . .

There are those who travel and those who are going somewhere. They are different and yet they are the same. The success has this over his rivals: he knows where he is going.
~ Mark Caine

. . . .

"Carpe Diem"- Seize the Day

Everything comes too late for those who only wait.
~ Elbert Hubbard

If what you are doing is not helping you to achieve your goal, you may have to make a radical change. Most of us know full well the change we need to make, but recoil from it because it will involve some sort of unpleasantness. Only when the frustration from not reaching our goal exceeds our desire to stay in our "comfort zone", will we make the necessary change.

For many years I thought that my goal of going to the Olympics would be achieved in the sport of water polo. I was a part of Newland's water polo program for ten years, and like many of his "boys" I felt a fierce loyalty towards him and the team. He'd been a second father to me, demanding but also gruffly affectionate, and under his coaching my play had improved so much that I was named to the first national water polo team in 1970. However, we had not played particularly well on our trip to Europe, and although I had worked my way off the bench to a starting position, my dream of making it to the Olympics seemed a long way off. To get to the Olympics in water polo I would have to be chosen for the team, and unless Newland was the coach I didn't think I had much of a chance. Also, at the age of 25 I knew I was on borrowed time as an athlete - back in those days it was difficult financially for anyone who wasn't in college to be training. So I was beginning to question the whole thing. To add to the pressure, I'd had one of those years crowded with major events: a new job, the birth of my daughter Alisha, and the unexpected death of my mother.

One night a friend of mine, Tony Ralphs, stopped by to see me, and presented me with an opportunity that would change my life. He had long been one of my idols, having been a record setting swimmer

· ·

When you determine what you want, you have made the most important decision of your life. You have to know what you want in order to attain it.
~ Douglas Lurtan

· · · · · · · · · · · · · ·

Don't let that which you cannot do, stop you from doing what you can do.
~ John Wooden

· · · · · · · · · · · · · ·

We are all faced with great opportunities – brilliantly disguised as impossible situations.
~ Albert Einstein

· ·

in high school and an Olympian in 1964 in the sport of kayaking. He had recently made a comeback and had set his sights on the '72 Olympics in Munich, and sensing my disillusionment with water polo he urged me to change my sport to kayaking. He was very excited and persuasive, and practically guaranteed that if I paddled with him we would both go to Munich. After kayaking with Tony several times, I was hooked on the sport. Naïvely, I believed that by switching to kayaking I could realize my Olympic dream and avoid all the politics of water polo at the same time. When I thought of the sacrifices I'd have to make, however, my heart sank. In essence, I would have to dump Newland and the rest of the team, and divorce myself from the program that had been my home for so long. I'd seen how much it hurt Newland when other athletes quit, and since I was the team captain and also one of the few left-handed players, I knew that he relied on me a lot. Leaving was going to be hard.

We are often set in our ways and comfortable with what is familiar, and change is difficult. I knew the sport of water polo inside out, and at the national level I knew all the players and coaches. Kayaking would be an entirely new sport for me, and what's more, I'd be training on my own. The decision to switch would affect my wife and father, too, for while they often came to watch me play water polo, kayaking is not a good spectator sport. Over the next few months, I agonized about what to do.

One day I found a letter from an artist friend of mine, Jeff Horn. In a moment of discouragement I had written to him and said how lucky he was that his talent would improve with age, while mine was limited to my youth. In his reply Jeff told me that because my talent was perishable, I should pursue my Olympic goal with total commitment, so that later on I would have no regrets. He said that with every decision there is a sacrifice to be made in some area, and he encouraged me to be brave enough to "seize the day" and take the opportunity to fulfill my potential.

Reading Jeff's letter again, it made perfect sense. His words gave me the boost I needed, and mustering all the courage I had I told Newland I was switching from water polo to kayaking. Although he had seen it coming, I know he felt betrayed. I could only hope he understood how urgent I felt it was to follow my dream.

. . . .

Every exit is an entry somewhere.
~ *Tom Stoppard*

. . . .

Some of us miss opportunity because we are
too dull to try. Others let opportunity go by,
too much startled when they see it to
take hold of it.
~ *Arthur Brisbane*

. . . .

Let not the opportunity that is so fleeting, yet
so full, pass neglected away.
~ *O. L. Frothingham*

. . . .

I did not regret my decision. In the summer of 1971 Tony and I qualified for the National Team and were off to Europe to train and race with some of the best, and in 1976 I finally reached my goal of going to the Olympics.

Whatever the change you have to make in order to reach your own goal, do it, for to get to the end of your life and wonder what might have been would be a tragedy. *BL*

. . . .

*Do not save your loving speeches for your
friends till they are dead. Do not write them on
their tombstones, speak them
rather now instead.*
~ *Anna Cummins*

. . . .

*I'm not a self-made man, I cannot forget
those who have sacrificed for me
to get where I am today.*
~ *Jessie Hill*

. . . .

*I keep my friends as misers do their treasure,
because, of all the things granted us by
wisdom, none is greater or better
than friendship.*
~ *Pietro Aretino*

. . . .

Surround Yourself with Success

*There is no such thing as a self-made man. You will reach your goal
only with the help of others.*
~ *George Shinn*

A distant clang of hammers was the only sound in the Olympic
Stadium as Julie and I ran down a ramp onto the deserted track. We
had arrived at the Olympic Village in Montreal a short time before and
had immediately put on our running shoes and jogged over to the stadium. In a few days time we would be marching in the opening ceremonies of the 17th Olympic Games and the stadium would be full of
noise and excitement. For now it was quiet, just a few workmen putting last minute touches to the facility, and we stood in awe on the
freshly surfaced track. This was the Olympics! We had made it; the
event that had dominated our lives for the past several years was about
to become a reality. We ran around the track several times and my
elation soon gave way to gratitude, for I knew I had not gotten to the
Olympics by myself. Looking up into the empty stands I saw in my
mind's eye row upon row of the friends, relatives, teammates and
coaches who had helped me get there, and I realized that one of the
crucial factors to success in anything is having the right people around.

My support group included my parents, who from the beginning
encouraged me, but never pushed me. They knew that playing a sport
is one of the best ways to gain self-respect and discipline, and they
came to all my swim meets and games. When I started training for the
Olympics, they never questioned the hours I was putting in, and I was
grateful for their support.

When you are with a group of people who have the same goals,
you can encourage each other and draw strength from each other, and

. . . .

No matter what accomplishments you make,
someone helped you.
~ *Althea Gibson*

. . . .

Kindness is the golden chain by which society
is bound together.
~ *Goethe*

. . . .

In a friend you find a second self.
~ *Isabelle Norton*

. . . .

it will be easier to stay committed. Kayaking brought Julie and me together when she was only 14 years old, and we trained together for hours each day. Five years later we ended up being the first married couple from the United States to compete in the same Olympics. Most of our friends were athletes, too, and even paddlers who came from Canada and Sweden to train in the perfect conditions that Newport Beach offered became part of our support group.

We knew how important it was to learn from someone who had done what we wanted to do. In our sport, Marcia Smoke was considered the Queen of Kayaking, having competed in three Olympic Games and won a bronze medal in 1964 in Tokyo. During the summers we were lucky enough to spend a week or two at her house on the St. Joseph River in Michigan, and we used to sit around and ask about her Olympic experiences. She would get out her scrapbook and her medal, and let us look at them. The medal was surprisingly heavy, as beautiful as an exquisite bronze sculpture. Turning it over and over in our hands, feeling every curve of the laurel wreath on the distinctive Greek goddess, we wondered what it was like to go to the Olympics. Marcia tried to tell us, but her voice trailed off and after a pause she said, "I can't exactly put it into words, you'll have to go yourself to find out." We were determined to. She made it real for us, and those long summer days of dreaming and discussion helped to crystallize our desire.

While Marcia prompted us to dream, others helped with the practical aspect of training. Never be too proud to ask for help when you need it. When my partner Mike Johnson and I began to run into problems, after more than two years of training together without a coach, Andras Szente agreed to step in. We needed someone to act as a buffer to our different personalities, and Julie, too, needed someone impartial to train her. Andras had been World Champion and a silver medallist for Hungary at the Rome Olympics in 1960, and in the months leading up to the Olympics he helped as much with the psychology of racing as he did with our workout schedule. Without him, I honestly doubt that we would have been jogging around the Olympic Stadium in Montreal, about to take part in an extraordinary world event.

A shout jolted me out of my reverie. From the empty seats a workman came hurrying down to the track and told us, in a thick French-Canadian accent, that we had to leave immediately. This was a con-

. . . .

True friendship is a plant of slow growth, and must undergo and withstand the shocks of adversity, before it is entitled to the appellation.
~ George Washington

. . . .

Without friends, no one would want to live, even if he had all other goods.
~ Aristotle

. . . .

Remember, the greatest gift is not found in a store nor under a tree, but in the hearts of true friends.
~ Cindy Lew

. . . .

struction area, and we had no hard hats. We thanked him with a smile, knowing that in just a few days we would be back.

The next time we ran down the ramp into the stadium we were met with a roar of cheers and shouts and a blast of color. Tens of thousands of people packed into the seats, waving wildly as each nation's flag was paraded around the track. Marcia was right: the feeling is impossible to describe. I was walking on air. Amazingly, as I looked toward the mass of faces in the stands the people I knew stood out. There were two water polo friends, Tom Hermstead and John Felix, waving, and our eyes met in recognition. There was Julie's family, all in a row, standing out as though they had fluorescent clothing on. My little son Billy, his face shining, was sitting next to my Dad. All the people closest to us, who had supported us throughout, were there. It was as though the connection could not be broken, even in a blur of a hundred thousand faces, and I will always be grateful to all of them. *BL*

. . . .

The greatest test of courage on earth is to bear defeat without losing heart.
~ *Robert Green Ingersoll*

. . . .

The excesses of our youth are checks written against our age, and they are payable with interest thirty years later.
~ *Charles Caleb Colton*

. . . .

He is not wise who is not wise for himself.
~ *Old English Proverb*

. . . .

Older and Wiser

*We deem those happy who from the experience of life have learned
to bear its ills, without being overcome by them.*
~ *Juvenal*

As young athletes, we tend to take our bodies for granted, often abusing them with not enough sleep, too much junk food, or too many hard workouts. We feel indestructible. If an injury occurs, we can ignore it and still recover because we have the resilience of youth. We little realize that when we run, swim or bike long distances it might one day catch up with us.

Until a few years ago every workout I did was a hard one. I rarely stretched and I could train right through any aches and pains. It was easy to tell other people to take days off if they felt an injury coming on, but I often ignored my own advice. For over ten years I followed a grueling training routine that allowed me to dominate the masters (over 40) age group in races. However, as I got older, things began to change. Twice I suffered injuries that prevented me from training, and I have to admit that the first time it happened, I didn't handle it very well.

In the summer of 1992 I was on vacation in Zion National Park, in Utah, a deep canyon of spectacular rust red cliffs and pine forests with a river meandering through the middle of it. I had been training hard for the Triathlon World Championships that year and one morning I set out to run along a steep switch-back trail overlooking the canyon. As I ran, the nagging thought that this was prime terrain for a twisted ankle crossed my mind, but nothing happened. With relief I saw the end of the trail and ironically, just as I started across a flat piece of land leading to the highway, my right foot twisted in the soft dirt. Pain shot through my ankle, and instantly I knew that this was one of those sprains

. . . .

Wisdom comes by disillusionment.
~ *George Santayana*

. . . .

You must work at playing hard with positive energy, not anger to fuel your desire to perform. You must work to learn to love the fight; when adversity strikes it means no retreating, no whining, no excusing, no raging. Competitive problems become stimulating rather than threatening and since positive emotion fuels the challenge response, a sense of loving the battle gradually takes form. To love winning is easy; to love the battle requires toughness. Responding to crisis, adversity, and pressure with a sense of challenge and love of the battle is neither common nor normal. Instead, it is the mark of a winner, a leader, a champion.
~ *James Loehr*

. . . .

that is worse than a break. Sitting in the doctor's office a few days later it occurred to me that maybe I wasn't invincible after all.

I tried to train through the injury, but I'd run for three or four miles and my foot would swell up so much that I couldn't see the anklebone, and I'd have to lay off for a few days. My times got worse and worse, and although I didn't realize it, I sank into a depression. When exercise is so much a part of your life, it is very difficult to accept inactivity. I kept telling myself that I'd be back to training the next week, and then the next week, but as the months went by my fitness level decreased and my motivation to exercise gradually slipped away. Before long I had to buy a set of fat-boy clothes to accommodate my flab, and without the discipline to cross train I lost a great cardiovascular base. I'd never been in worse shape; I ended up disliking myself and feeling totally miserable. Eventually, the ankle sprain required surgery, and the recovery period only added to my frustration and my waistline.

It seems that one of the challenges of getting older is being more susceptible to injury and taking longer to heal. This is just a fact of life. But when faced with a setback we always have a choice: either we give in to the situation, or we get creative and find a way to lift ourselves out of the depression. From experience I knew that setting goals has always motivated me to action, so I decided to aim for the World Championships in 1996. It seemed like a realistic goal: I would be 50 years old and in a new age group, and I would have two years to get back into shape. I began to train hard and see results, and as soon as I had a purpose again my whole attitude towards life improved.

I was working my way back into the best shape I'd been in for several years, when I was injured yet again. Riding hard one afternoon along Laguna Canyon Road, I crashed my bike and broke my right shoulder. At first I was angry and frustrated that this had happened so soon after my last injury, but then I realized that this time I knew how to handle it. I vowed to be patient with myself and be sensible about letting my shoulder heal, but to maintain my level of fitness. Within a week I was exercising as best I could without using my arm: riding a stationary bike, running in the pool, and even swimming with my right arm strapped to my side. It worked. Mentally and physically I came out of 1995 in pretty good shape, full of high hopes and energy and

. . . .

If youth knew; if age could.
~ *Henri Estienne*

. . . .

The most important thing in life is not the triumph but the struggle. The essential thing is not to have conquered but to have fought well.
~ *Baron Pierre de Coubertin*

. . . .

The doors of wisdom are never shut.
~ *Ben Franklin*

. . . .

chomping at the bit to turn fifty and prove myself again on the race course.

There has to be some advantage to growing older, and I believe that we are given a new perspective to replace the arrogance of youth. We have the experience to make sensible decisions, which can help us stay healthy and competitive. My two injuries humbled me and taught me to respect my body's limits, and more importantly, I learned how to handle setbacks. Injuries are inevitable, but as we mature we can deal with them in a positive way, realizing that with proper care we'll recover.

My shoulder healed well, and my patience was rewarded with a great season in which I won the World Championship title I had been aiming for. I'll never have the strength and speed of my early forties again, but in the process of getting older I've acquired a lot of experience and a little bit of wisdom, both of which have been much more valuable to me than a fistful of medals could ever be. *BL*

Chapter Twelve

Self-Respect

. . . .

Competing in sports has taught me that if I'm not willing to give 120%, somebody else will.
~ *Ron Blomberg*

. . . .

A young person, to achieve, must first get out of his mind any notion either of the ease or the rapidity of success. Nothing ever just happens in this world.
~ *Edward William Bok*

. . . .

They who lack talent expect things to happen without effort. They ascribe failure to a lack of inspiration or ability, or to misfortune, rather than to insufficient application.
At the core of every true talent there is an awareness of the difficulties inherent in any achievement, and the confidence that comes by persistence and patience in something worthwhile will be realized. Thus talent is a species of vigor.
~ *Eric Hoffer*

. . . .

Hard Work Begets Talent

Skill to do comes of doing.
~ *Ralph Waldo Emerson*

I've always said that it doesn't really matter how talented you are, as long as you're prepared to work. Hard work begets talent, in my opinion. Andy Nott, a player on my water polo team several years ago, is a good example.

Andy had been playing water polo for me for a while and was about to enter his senior year in college. He wasn't a big kid, maybe a tad under 6 feet, and he was not super-talented, but I knew he was hoping to be my starting goalie that year. I liked and respected Andy, and since I figure it's always better to be honest with people and not jerk them around, I told him the truth: although he had worked very hard and had come a long way with the amount of athletic ability he possessed, I didn't think he was good enough to be my starting goalie. I told him there was nothing to like or dislike about the decision, it was just a fact of life. He was very emotional about the whole thing, almost broke down and cried, and I wondered if he would quit the program.

I should have known better. Mentally, Andy's a pretty tough kid. He knew what he had to do and he did it. He made a decision, stayed out there, and kept working really hard. He made no excuses; just put more time into everything. The weight room, the workouts, he did what he needed to do. Andy was always liked by his teammates, but now they respected him even more. He obviously felt good about what he was doing too. The harder he played, the more confidence he gained, and he kept on getting better. I'll never forget the smile on his face when I let him know how impressed I was with what he had accomplished, and told him he'd earned the starting goalie position.

. . . .

Adversity has the effect of eliciting talents, which, in prosperous circumstances, would have lain dormant.

~ Horace

. . . .

Men who have attained things worth having in this world have worked while others idled, have persevered while others gave up in despair, have practiced early in life the valuable habits of self-denial, industry, and singleness of purpose. As a result, they enjoy in later life the success so often erroneously attributed to good luck.

~ Grenville Kleiser

. . . .

Success is simply a matter of good luck. Ask any failure.

~ Earl Wilson

. . . .

Andy had an extremely successful year. To himself he proved that when confronted with an obstacle he didn't just roll over and die, and to me he proved that hard work does indeed beget talent. *EHN*

Although I was disappointed, Newland's words made me think. I realized I had a choice: either I could quit, or I could work my ass off and push my athletic and mental abilities to the limit and try to improve. It was up to me. Fortunately I chose the latter, and what a great experience it was. What a challenge! It was probably the biggest growing experience of my adult life. I learned about the self-respect that comes from struggling with our weaknesses and overcoming them, about fighting hard. I learned that I had a strength in me that I could apply to other situations, and the feeling of self worth that came from that time helped shape me into the person I am today. Most of my trophies are gathering dust in the garage, but the letter Newland wrote me after I made it to the championships is still in my top desk drawer.
~ Andy Nott, U.C.I Water Polo 1987-90

. . . .

***Better to die on one's feet than to live
on one's knees***
~ Dolores Ibarruri

. . . .

You are never a loser until you quit trying.
~ Mike Ditka

. . . .

***Courage and perseverance have a magical
talisman, before which difficulties disappear
and obstacles vanish into air.***
~ John Quincy Adams

. . . .

The Pride Lasts Longer Than the Pain

*We are made to persist. That's how we find
out what we are.*
~ Tobias Wolff

I've seen how sport brings out the best in people. It is one of the few things in our comfortable lives in middle class America that can take us to "the edge", that place where we can face the negative, weak part of our character. It's where we can feel the fear or the desire to quit, and find out who we are and what we are capable of. We're challenged and tested in sport, and each time we don't quit we get stronger mentally. The self-respect we achieve by facing a challenge and not giving in, or by setting a goal and working towards it, will last a lifetime.

"The pride lasts longer than the pain," declared the slight woman standing in front of my triathlon class one spring night in 1996. Jill Newman was a member of the triathlon club I belonged to, and having heard her story I knew there was a valuable lesson to be shared with the students I was teaching at the time. She was sharing the mantra that she repeated to herself as she ran up the final hill of the Wildflower Triathlon in central California. Determined to finish the race, even with her left shoe saturated with blood from a broken blister and her body drooping with exhaustion from the intense heat, she knew that when it was over, the agony of those last moments would be swept away by the thrill of achievement. She had trained for months for this race, and she was not about to quit. So she dug deep, mustered up every ounce of courage she possessed, and struggled on to the rhythm of her chant, " The pride lasts longer than the pain, the pride lasts longer than the pain".

. . . .

Many of life's failures are people who did not
realize how close they were to success when
they gave up.
~ *Thomas Edison*

. . . .

Bear in mind, if you are going to amount to
anything, that your success does not depend
upon the brilliance and the impetuosity with
which you take hold, but upon the everlasting
and sanctified bull doggedness after you hang
on and have taken hold.
~ *Dr A. B. Meldrum*

. . . .

He who loses wealth loses much; he who loses
a friend loses more; but he who loses
courage loses all.
~ *Miguel De Cervantes*

. . . .

Not only did Jill finish the race that day, she also won her age group division, placing third overall. As she was telling her story I could see it was having quite an effect on my college students. They sat in silence, listening to the calm voice of this unassuming athlete who obviously had the spirit of a tiger. Jill could have quit that day, but she didn't. She knew that while the blisters would heal within a few weeks and the heat would soon be just an unpleasant memory, the self respect and confidence she would gain by hanging on would forever be a part of her character.

It was no surprise to hear that at the end of the summer she was invited to train in Colorado Springs as one of the first members of the U.S. National Triathlon Team, with the goal of being a member of the 2000 Olympic Team. To do this she had to give up a lucrative position in a law firm, but it was a small sacrifice to be able to follow her dream. For the next four years she was one of the highest ranked Americans on the international scene.

About a month before the Olympic Trials in Texas, Jill pulled a muscle in her leg. True to character, she decided to race anyway, and she finished tenth, not high enough to qualify for the team. Afterwards, she said she had no regrets. Disappointment, yes, but she knew the journey she'd embarked on had no guarantees, and she'd fulfilled her goal of being the best that she could be. In the end, that is what counts.

Athletes like Jill help us realize that the only limits we have are in our mind. I know she influenced my students that night, and as they face inevitable struggles in their lives they will surely remember her words: "the pride lasts longer than the pain". *BL*

. . . .

We need to find the courage to say "No!" to the things and people that are not serving us if we want to rediscover ourselves and live our lives with authenticity.
~ *Barbara DeAngelis*

. . . .

We become just by performing just actions, temperate by performing temperate actions, brave by performing brave actions.
~ *Aristotle*

. . . .

The real acid test of courage is to be just your honest self when everybody is trying to be like somebody else.
~ *Andrew Jensen*

. . . .

The Courage to Move On

Courage is the power to let go of the familiar.
~ Mary Bryant

Change is always difficult. To leave the secure and the familiar behind takes courage, but I've learned that when we make a change because it is in our own best interest, we gain a lot of self-respect.

When my wife Julie was involved in triathlons, her specialty was the ultra-distance races. She had the physical strength to excel in each of the three disciplines: swimming, biking and running, and she had the mental strength not to quit when the going got tough. In fact, the longer and harder the race, the better she seemed to perform. In May 1982 she fractured the tibia in her left leg in a bike accident, but undaunted she carried on training. She competed in the Hawaiian Ironman that October, winning the women's race in record time and proving herself a top tri-athlete. Within weeks she was racing again, and at the inaugural triathlon in Nice, France she finished fourth.

A short while later, the J. David Triathlon team offered Julie and me sponsorship, and we accepted. It was never Julie's goal to be a professional or to become famous. She enjoyed competing and was an accomplished athlete, and the sponsorship was a welcome financial relief for us at the time. We would each get $1500 a month, all flights and entry fees to races, bike maintenance, and a bonus scale based on our performance. Considering we had to pay for just about everything when we were kayakers, this was a dream come true. It looked like the beginning of a great season.

However, there is a big difference between racing for fun, and racing under the obligation of a sponsorship. The pressure to perform was intense. Having demonstrated her ability, Julie was expected to be

· ·

Whatever course you decide upon, there is
always someone to tell you that you are wrong.
There are always difficulties arising which
tempt you to believe that your critics are right.
To map out a course of action and follows it to
an end requires...courage.
~ *Ralph Waldo Emerson*

· · · · · · · · · · · · · ·

Courage is the first of human qualities
because it is the quality which
guarantees all others.
~ *Winston Churchill*

· · · · · · · · · · · · · ·

Give me the fortitude to endure the things
which cannot be changed, and the courage to
change the things which should be changed,
and the wisdom to know one from the other.
~ *Oliver J. Hart*

· ·

at peak performance in every race, and she wanted to live up to the expectations of her sponsors. She participated in quite a few races that year, too many, including three ultra-distance races and a couple of half-Ironmans which she won handily. In spite of her success, people would talk. If she had an "off" day, they would speculate why, and there was once a magazine article that referred to her as "an out-of-shape Julie Leach", even though she finished third in the race. Always conscientious, Julie felt that if she didn't win, she had let her sponsors down. The pressure seemed to increase with every race. After a few months her enthusiasm began to wane, and when housework began to seem more appealing than training, it was definitely a sign of burnout.

One day it came to a head. We often trained together, but on this particular day Julie didn't want to go out and do our bike ride, so I went by myself. When I got home there was a letter waiting for me. In the letter, Julie said that although triathlon was her job and she owed a lot to her sponsors, she had reached a point in her athletic career when she knew it was time to move on. She had achieved many of her goals and now simply had lost the desire to train and compete at a level that put her at the cutting edge of the sport. She was putting her decision in writing to me so that she wouldn't back down, for the decision was a tremendously difficult one to make.

I was used to seeing Julie's character in competition, and I could tell that what she had to do now was harder, much harder, than not quitting during a race. It took great courage for her to step away from something that had totally filled her life, especially since she didn't know what she would do next.

Interestingly, she later received letters and phone calls from several triathletes who commended her on the decision to withdraw from competitive sport while at the top, and wished, almost wistfully, that they too had the courage to make a change. *BL*

• •

Self-respect permeates every
aspect of your life.
~ *Joe Clark*

• • • • • • • • • • • • • •

A person's worth is contingent upon who he
is, not upon what he does, or how much he
has. The worth of a person, or a thing, or an
idea, is in being, not in doing, not in having.
~ *Alice Mary Hilton*

• • • • • • • • • • • • • •

Until you make peace with who you are, you'll
never be content with what you have.
~ *Doris Mortma*

• •

A Circle of Success

The mediocre teacher tells. The good teacher explains. The superior teacher demonstrates. The great teacher inspires.
~ *William A. Ward*

Those of us who played on Newland's water polo team will never forget him. He was focused, intense, and more demanding than any teacher I've known. Every detail of our mental and physical performance concerned him, and we knew he expected us to be as strong in character as we were physically. Yes, we could bench press 300lbs, but could we get to practice on time? Perhaps we were masters at flinging the ball into the net from the other side of the pool during a game, but did we have the self-discipline to get up at 5 a.m. day after day even when it was cold outside or we were tired? He wanted us to be mentally tough, and I for one can say that most of the things I learned about life, I learned not in kindergarten, but in Newland's water polo program.

In the middle of a workout he often commanded us to stop and listen, and we would tread water or sit along the wall of the weight room while he talked to us about something he felt was important. I remember one day he asked if we knew the difference between pride and self-respect. Seeing our puzzled looks, he began to explain. As he saw it, the difference between pride and self-respect was a subtle but crucial one. Pride, he said, is a feeling of satisfaction that comes from the achievement of someone or something we feel attached to, such as when a favorite team wins a championship or beats a rival. We can take pride in going to a certain school, or belonging to a certain team. But pride is not essential to building character.

Self-respect is different. Newland has always been passionate about the need for self-respect. Defined as "a sense of one's own dignity and

. . . .

*We must view young people not as empty
bottles to be filled, but as candles to be lit.*
~ Robert H. Shaffer

. . . .

*While we are indifferent to our good qualities,
we keep on deceiving ourselves in regard to
our faults, until we come to look
on them as virtues.*
~ Heinrich Heine

. . . .

*Flatter me, and I may not believe you, criticize
me and I may not like you, ignore me and I
may not forgive you, encourage me and
I may not forget you.*
~ William Arthur

. . . .

integrity", we earn self-respect day after day by what we do. While pride can come from just watching something, self-respect cannot. Whether our goal is a fitness goal such as getting into shape, or a challenge like quitting smoking, we are all very much the same: we only gain true self-respect by setting a goal and achieving it. Achieving a goal gives us a burst of confidence, which in turn leads to a willingness to set more goals; reaching these new goals gives us even more self-respect and more confidence, and we aim higher still. It is a circle of success.

While the sweat dried in salty streaks on our skin, we sat and listened to Newland, and I have never forgotten the significance of his words. As a teacher, over the past 30 years I've seen the "self-esteem" movement become part of our educational and parenting philosophy, and in my opinion we are way off mark. Not reprimanding children when they misbehave for fear of hurting their egos, or trying to instill self-respect by means of unconditional praise or grade inflation in schools, have all too often resulted in rude, arrogant and spoiled brats.

It is our responsibility as parents to teach our children. The best way to do that is to set an example. If we have the self-discipline to work out when we don't feel like it, or the will to carry on when we are tired, we will encourage them to persist when their own path gets tough. Newland used to stress that playing a sport is one of the best ways of earning self-respect because the feedback is immediate, but even the simplest actions such as writing a term paper and turning it in on time, or keeping a bedroom clean, can lead to self-respect. If we are not afraid of a challenge, and we go the extra mile in terms of effort, self-respect can be gained even in failure. The one thing that matters is that the effort has been valiant. That is what we need to teach our children, and maybe then we will see the emotionally mature, appreciative and confident young adults we had envisioned. *BL*

I realized early on that I was more effective as a teacher on the pool deck than in the classroom. Out in the open, the kids would listen to me. I could talk about the qualities I felt were important in a man, and they would remember. Many players come back and tell me that most of what has been useful in their lives was learned while they were part of my water polo program. That makes me feel good.
~ *Ted Newland*

Chronology: Bill Leach

Born 1946, Glendale, Ca.

1960-62 Newport Harbor High School, California

1962-64 Corona del Mar High School, California: All CIF Water Polo Team; All American Swimming Team (400 freestyle); 1st Athlete of the Year.

1964-65 Orange Coast College, Costa Mesa, California: All-American Swimming Team

1965-68 University of California, Irvine: AAU Outdoor National Champions in Water Polo; NCAA All-American in Swimming & Water Polo

1966 Married Bonnie Black (divorced 1974)

1967 Birth of son: William Braxton

1969 AAU Indoor National Champions in Water Polo

1970 AAU Outdoor National Champions; U.S. National Water Polo Team (toured Europe)

1971 Birth of daughter: Alisha Tay

1971-79 U.S. National Kayak Team & National Champion;

1975 Married Julie Jones

1976 U.S. Olympic Kayak Team (Montreal)

1977-83 Corona del Mar H.S. Girls Cross Country Co-Coach with wife Julie

1980-present: Triathlons (over 200 races); U.S. National Masters Triathlon Champion (1986-90); 2nd in ITU Triathlon World Championship, Masters 40+ division (Avignon, France); 6th in ITU Triathlon World Championships, 45-49 age group(Moskoka, Canada); 1996 World Champion 50-54 age group ITU Triathlon World Championships (Clevland, Ohio)

1981 Tahiti International Outrigger Champions

1982 Molokai Outrigger World Champions (Koa Boats)

1985 Inducted into UC Irvine Hall of Fame

1988 Birth of son: Shane Hayden

1991-97 Irvine Valley College Cross Country Co-Coach with wife Julie

1993 Birth of son: Hayden Anders Jones

1998 World Masters Games Champions in Water Polo 50+ (Portland, Oregon)

Chronology: Ted Newland

Born 1927, California

1929 Father died

1951-52 Air Force, San Antonio, Texas

1954 Graduated from Occidental College

1955 Grad School

1955 Started teaching history at Newport Harbor High School, California

1962-1966 Teacher at Corona del Mar High School, California

1965 CIF Water Polo Championship coach

1966 to present – U.C.I Water Polo coach

Coaching record: Won 3 Div II NCAA Swimming Championship 1969-70-71 Has been in 21 of 31 NCAA Water Polo Championships; has the most wins in NCAA Water Polo history. Current record: 663 wins, 288 losses, 5 ties. NCAA Water Polo Champions: 1970,1982,1989. Coached 64 All American players. 12 athletes became Olympians. National coach for Pan Am Games, 1971 (gold medal) and 1974. Head coach of the World University Games in 1973 (Russia), 1979 (Bulgaria), 1991 (Great Britain), 1995 (Japan), 1999 (Spain). Has coached in over 5,300 water polo games and swim meets.

About the Authors

Bill Leach

Leach has taught History at Corona del Mar High School since 1969. As well as working out regularly, and writing this book, he has been the Race Director of the Pacific Coast Triathlon, which he co-founded in 1998. He lives with his wife Julie and their sons Shane and Hayden in Irvine, California.

Ted Newland

Newland has spent much of his life on the pool deck, and is about to begin his 36th year of coaching water polo at U.C. Irvine. In his words, " It's been fun, and I would do it all over again if I could". He works out daily to stay up with his team. Newland lives in Costa Mesa, California, with his wife Anne. He has three grown children.

Lesley Bindloss

Lesley grew up in England, where she earned a B.A. degree in English Literature at the University of Southampton. She moved to California in 1984, and she now runs and writes in Irvine, where she lives with her husband Keith and two children,Emma and Chris.

Bill Leach and Ted Newland are available for speaking engagements; please contact Lynne Chapman at (949) 798-0708 for further information.

Circle of Success
Order Form

· · · · · · · · · · · · · · ·

Only $19.95

includes shipping, sales tax and handling

· ·

Name _____

Address_____

City_____

State_____   Zip _____

Quanity_____ @ $19.95 Total _____

                                               Total _____

· ·

Mail to: Hawthorne Hills Publishers
            P. O. Box 5209
            Irvine, CA 92616

Visit our website : www.circleofsuccess.net